# Super Simple
# Air Fryer Baking

# Super Simple
# Air Fryer Baking

## 60 Favourite Bakes Perfect for Air Fryers

*Hardie Grant*

BOOKS

**Katy Greenwood**

Photography by Ant Duncan

# CONTENTS

# Introduction

If you are reading this, I'm sure you are familiar with the wonder that is air fryer cooking, but I can't wait to show you how fantastically easy baking in an air fryer can be. When I first got my air fryer, I initially just used it to prepare the usual family friendly meals that need to be on the table instantly (think fries and nuggets – such a breeze when it only takes 5 minutes to cook!) and for cooking those little party food bits and bobs you buy for a picking plate, like spring rolls and chicken wings, but after a while I realised I wasn't maximising its potential. I decided to experiment and turned to my favourite sweet treat – scones – and found that my air fryer turned out a perfect bake in just 10 minutes. Even better, it made it so simple to throw together a small batch bake – I never want to make more than 8 scones because they need to be eaten while they're fresh, and this way I had a British cream tea in an instant! I love making small batches of cookies in the air fryer too, I just bake the few I know will be eaten and pop the rest in the refrigerator or freezer to bake another time. You'll find plenty of other recipes in the following pages that make life in the kitchen quicker and easier.

One of the other benefits of using the air fryer is of course that it is typically cheaper to run than a large oven. My air fryer, according to the manufacturer, uses 80 per cent less energy than a traditional oven. I also love that the air fryer turns itself off when the time is up. So, if for some reason you don't hear the beep to say it has finished, it doesn't matter as your bakes won't be over done – exactly what we all need when we are juggling a few different tasks!

It's my mission to show how this brilliant little machine can produce stand-out bakes that are cheaper, easier and quicker than traditional oven recipe counterparts – I hope you enjoy the bakes in this book as much as I do.

# TIPS AND TRICKS

**Whilst testing the recipes for this book I spotted a few things that might snag your perfect air fryer bakes:**

When lining your baking tins with baking parchment, make sure that you cut it so it doesn't come too high above the top of the tin, I'd say no more than 0.5 cm (¼ in). This is so that the parchment doesn't flap around in the breeze of the air fryer fan and inhibit your bakes, but also because any long edges can catch on the heating element.

With loaf tins, I found that using parchment loaf tin liners, rather than baking parchment worked really well, as these don't tend to come up too high and are a little less faff.

When baking cakes and breads, you'll need to remove any racks or baskets in the air fryer, so that the bakes don't rise and connect with the element (which I can confirm is messy and annoying!).

When baking cookies, I usually put these on baking parchment in the base (not on the rack) of the air fryer. Make sure that you place cookies on the edge of it, to hold it down so that you don't get funny shaped cookies! You could use non-stick silicone mats for this if you like, as they're thicker and don't flap around, however I found that the base of the cookies didn't bake quite as well when using these.

# Choosing an air fryer

For this book, I chose a 5.7-litre (6 quart) air fryer with only one drawer; this was because the drawer was square and so would fit in a large variety of sizes of baking tin, from a 900 g (2 lb) loaf tin, up to a 23 cm (9 in) springform cake tin. I don't have a huge kitchen, so the square size also meant that it didn't take up too much space on my worktop, leaving me room to work next to it.

If you want to use the air fryer for baking, I'd go for one that has a baking function. You don't have to, but I find it does work slightly better since it tames the power of the fan, meaning things are blown about a little less. Usually, air fryers with a baking function come with other useful settings too like grill, roast, reheat and even dehydrate, which makes the machine even more useful in the kitchen.

# Recipe Notes

I tested these recipes in a 5.7-litre (6 quart) air fryer with one drawer. As air fryers can vary you may find you need to bake things for a minute or two more or less here and there.

As ever with baking, accuracy of measurement is key. When I refer to tablespoon or teaspoon measures, these are always level.

Butter is unsalted unless I specify in the recipe (for some bakes salted butter works best).

Milk is whole (full-fat) unless stated otherwise.

Cream cheese is full-fat unless stated otherwise.

All eggs are medium for these recipes, unless I say to use large eggs.

When I use dark chocolate, I have just used easily accessible 54 per cent cocoa solids chocolate. If you prefer chocolate with a higher cocoa solids content, then of course feel free to use it.

I tend to use a hand-held electric whisk for the baking in this book, as most recipes are fairly small, however if you have a stand mixer then that will also work.

When I say grease and line the base of a tin, you should grease the whole tin, but only line the base. This is because the baking parchment often flops over and inhibits the rising of the bake. Greasing the sides should be sufficient to make the sides of the bake not stick, but if they do slightly, then just run a knife around the edges to release.

In a few of the recipes in this book I've said to cover the bakes with foil, this is to prevent them browning too much. I didn't find overbrowning much of a problem with my air fryer, however since they are all a little different you may find your bakes (mostly things like cakes or breads) are browning a little too quickly. If this is the case then cover them with foil, making sure that the foil is tightly attached to the edge of any tins or underneath the bake itself, to prevent the foil being blown off into the element.

# CAKES

# Victoria Sponge

It's just as easy to make this classic in an air fryer – you'll just need to bake the sponges consecutively, rather than at the same time. The short wait time between bakes doesn't make any difference to the rise on the second cake, and it gives you a moment to tackle the very minimal washing up.

/ Serves 10 /

Grease and line the bases of two 20 cm (18 in) sandwich cake tins with baking parchment. Add the butter and caster sugar to a large bowl, and using a hand-held whisk, cream until light and fluffy. Beat in the eggs one by one, adding the vanilla with the last egg. Add the flour and whisk gently until combined. Divide the batter evenly between the prepared cake tins.

Heat the air fryer to 160°C (325°F). Once hot, bake the cakes, one at a time for 25 minutes. Leave to cool in the tin for a few minutes, before turning out onto a wire rack and leaving to cool completely.

Once the cakes are cool, in a medium bowl, whip the cream until just thickened. Place one of the cakes on a serving plate and spread the jam over the top, then dollop on the whipped cream and top with the second cake. Dust with icing sugar to serve.

175 g (6 oz) unsalted butter, softened, or baking spread
175 g (6 oz/¾ cup) caster (superfine) sugar
3 eggs
½ teaspoon vanilla extract
175 g (6 oz/scant 1½ cups) self-raising (self-rising) flour
200 ml (7 fl oz/scant 1 cup) double (heavy) or whipping cream
4 tablespoons raspberry or strawberry jam
icing (powdered) sugar, for dusting

# Carrot Cake

When deciding recipes for this book I asked friends what their favourite cake was and carrot cake was overwhelmingly the most popular choice, so of course I had to include it!

/ Cuts into 10 /

Grease and line the base of a 20 cm (8 in) springform cake tin (pan) with baking parchment.

Add the oil, orange juice and zest, brown sugar and eggs to a large bowl and beat together until well mixed. Sift all the dry ingredients into the wet along with the grated carrot and fold everything together gently.

Heat the air fryer to 160°C (325°F). Once hot, spoon the batter into the prepared tin and bake for 45–50 minutes or until a skewer inserted into the middle comes out clean. Leave to cool in the tin for 5 minutes, then turn out onto a wire rack and leave to cool completely.

Once the cake is cool, in a large bowl, beat the cream cheese, butter and icing sugar together until smooth. Transfer the cake to a serving plate or stand, then spread the cream cheese icing over the top of the cake. Top with orange zest, if you like.

150 ml (5 fl oz/scant ⅔ cup) vegetable oil, plus a little extra for greasing
zest and juice of 1 orange
200 g (7 oz/generous 1 cup) soft light brown sugar
3 eggs
200 g (7 oz/1⅔ cups) self-raising (self-rising) flour
½ teaspoon bicarbonate of soda (baking soda)
1 teaspoon ground cinnamon
½ teaspoon ground nutmeg
200 g (7 oz/1½ cups) grated carrot

FOR THE ICING (FROSTING)
280 g (10 oz/1¼ cups) cream cheese, at room temperature
125 g (4½ oz) butter, softened
125 g (4½ oz/1 cup) icing (powdered) sugar
orange zest, for topping (optional)

# Swirled Birthday Cake with Sprinkles

Whether you're a child or a grown up, nothing beats a bright and brash birthday cake, topped lavishly with creamy icing (frosting), a plethora of sprinkles and as many candles as you'll admit to! Use any food colourings you desire to create your favourite colourways.

/ Cuts into 16 /

Grease a square 20 cm (8 in) cake tin (pan) and line with baking parchment.

Add all the ingredients, except for the food colourings to a food processor and whizz until smooth. Transfer half of the batter from the food processor to another separate bowl. Add one of the food colours to the bowl and the other colour to the batter in the food processor and mix in until incorporated. Spoon a blob of each batter, one by one, on top of each other into the centre of the prepared cake tin.

Heat the air fryer to 160°C (325°F). Once hot, bake the cake for 35 minutes, or until risen and golden and a skewer inserted into the centre comes out clean. Leave to cool in the tin for a few minutes, then turn out onto a wire rack and leave to cool completely.

Once the cake is cool, in a large bowl, beat the butter until creamy, then gradually beat in the icing sugar and finally, the vanilla and boiling water. Keep beating for 2 minutes, or until the icing is fluffy. Spread over the top of the cake and decorate with sprinkles and, of course, birthday candles!

200 g (7 oz) soft unsalted butter or baking spread
200 g (7 oz/generous ¾ cup) caster (superfine) sugar
200 g (7 oz/1⅓ cups) self-raising (self-rising) flour
3 eggs
1 teaspoon baking powder
100 ml (3½ fl oz/scant ½ cup) milk
2 teaspoons vanilla extract
2 x 15 g (½ oz) tubes gel food colouring, (I used pink and green)
sprinkles and birthday candles, to decorate

FOR THE ICING (FROSTING)
150 g (5½ oz) unsalted butter, softened
300 g (10½ oz/scant 2½ cups) icing (powdered) sugar
1 teaspoon vanilla extract
2 teaspoons boiling water

# Red Velvet Cupcakes

With a light, fluffy texture and deliciously sweet icing (frosting), these perennially popular cupcakes will steal the heart of anyone you bake them for.

**/ Makes 6 /**

Line six individual mini pudding basins with the cupcake cases.

Add the oil and caster sugar to a large bowl and beat together until combined. Beat in the egg followed by the food colouring, lemon juice and vanilla. Add enough food colouring to make the mix nice and red, or as red as you'd like it!

Sift the flour, cocoa and bicarbonate of soda together into a small bowl. Beat half of the dry ingredients into the wet, then add half the yoghurt. Repeat until the dry ingredients and yoghurt have been incorporated and the batter is well mixed. Divide the batter between the prepared cupcake cases.

Heat the air fryer to 160°C (325°F). Once hot, bake the cupcakes for 25 minutes. Leave to cool in the moulds for a few minutes or until you're able to handle them, then turn out onto a wire rack and leave to cool completely.

Once the cupcakes are cool, slice 0.5 cm (¼ in) of the tops from the cupcakes, crumble into crumbs and set aside. In a large bowl, beat the butter until soft, then gradually beat in the cream cheese, followed by the icing sugar. Spoon into a piping bag fitted with a large star nozzle and pipe on top of the cupcakes. Sprinkle the tops with the crumbled cake and serve.

125 ml (4 fl oz/½ cup) vegetable oil
125 g (4½ oz/½ cup) caster (superfine) sugar
1 egg
1–2 x 15 g (½ oz) tubes red gel food colouring
½ teaspoon lemon juice
½ teaspoon vanilla extract
125 g (4½ oz/1 cup) plain (all-purpose) flour
1½ tablespoons cocoa (unsweetened cocoa) powder
½ teaspoon bicarbonate of soda (baking soda)
100 g (3½ oz) natural (plain) yoghurt

TO DECORATE
75 g (2½ oz) unsalted butter, softened
100 g (3½ oz/scant ½ cup) full-fat cream cheese, room temperature
225 g (8 oz/generous 1¾ cups) icing (powdered) sugar

# Coffee and Walnut Cake

When I was testing the recipes for this book there was so much cake at home that I was taking slices as gifts wherever I went. The coffee cake made it to my hairdressers. Their reaction when they tasted it made me realise it was a keeper, so here it is!

/ Cuts into 10 /

Grease and line the base of an 18 cm (7 in) springform cake tin (pan) with baking parchment.

Add the espresso powder to a small cup, then pour in the boiling water and leave to cool slightly.

Add the walnuts to a food processor and pulse to chop fairly finely, then add 2 tablespoons of the coffee and the remaining ingredients and whizz until smooth.

Spoon the batter into the prepared tin and smooth the top.

Heat the air fryer to 160°C (325°F). Once hot, bake the cake for 35 minutes, or until a skewer inserted into the centre comes out clean. Remove from the air fryer and, using the skewer, prick holes all over the top. Pour over all of the remaining coffee and leave the cake to cool in the tin for 5 minutes. Turn the cake out onto a wire rack and leave to cool completely.

Once the cake is cool, beat the butter, in a mixing bowl, until soft, then gradually beat in the icing sugar and the espress powder until fluffy. Swirl this over the cooled cake and dot the walnut halves around the edge.

125 g (4½ oz) unsalted butter, softened, or baking spread, plus extra for greasing
1 teaspoon espresso coffee powder
3 tablespoons boiling water
30 g (1 oz/¼ cup) walnuts
150 g (5½ oz/1¼ cups) self-raising (self-rising) flour
125 g (4½ oz/½ cup) caster (superfine) sugar
¼ teaspoon baking powder
2 eggs
1 teaspoon vanilla extract

FOR THE ICING (FROSTING)
75 g (2½ oz) unsalted butter
150 g (5 oz/1⅓ cup) icing (powdered) sugar
1 teaspoon espresso powder
10 walnut halves

# Plant-based Chocolate Cupcakes

These cupcakes are so good you'll want to make them again and again, whether you follow a plant-based diet or not.

/ Makes 6 /

Line six individual mini pudding basins with silicone cupcake cases.

Add the oat milk, melted butter, vinegar and vanilla extract to a jug and stir until combined.

Leave to stand for a few minutes. The mixture will look curdled but don't worry.

Add all the dry ingredients to another bowl and whisk in the oat milk mixture. Spoon the batter evenly into the cupcake cases.

Heat the air fryer to 160°C (325°F). Once hot, bake the cupcakes for 15 minutes. Leave to cool.

Once the cupcakes are cool, in a large bowl, beat the butter until creamy, then gradually whisk in the icing sugar and cocoa, adding a splash of oat milk to loosen the icing, if needed. Spoon and swirl or pipe the icing on the top of the cupcakes.

125 ml (4 fl oz/½ cup) oat milk
40 g (1½ oz) plant-based butter, melted
2 teaspoons cider vinegar
1 teaspoon vanilla extract
100 g (3½ oz/generous ¾ cup) plain (all-purpose) flour
100 g (3½ oz/½ cup) soft light brown sugar
3 tablespoons cocoa (unsweetened cocoa) powder
1 teaspoon baking powder

FOR THE ICING (FROSTING)
50 g (1¾ oz) plant-based butter, softened
75 g (2½ oz/⅔ cup) icing (powdered) sugar
25 g (1 oz/¼ cup) cocoa (unsweetened cocoa) powder
splash of oat milk (optional)

# Christmas Cake

I've only recently become a fan of things made with dried fruits. When I was younger I'd never have touched Christmas cake or mince pies, but these days I look forward to baking these Christmas treats. This cake, fragrant with orange and Earl Grey, is one I'll be making every year.

**/ Cuts into 16 /**

Add the mixed dried fruit and orange zest and juice to a large bowl, then pour over the tea. Cover and leave to soak overnight.

The next day, butter an 18 cm (7 in) springform cake tin (pan) and line with two layers of baking parchment.

Add the butter and sugar to a large bowl and beat together until creamy. Beat in the eggs, one by one, then stir in the flour, baking powder and spices until all the ingredients are well mixed. Add the soaked fruit and any liquid along with the flaked almonds and glacé cherries. Mix together then turn into the prepared cake tin. Smooth the top, then create a small dip in the middle of the cake (this should ensure a flat, rather than domed cake).

Heat the air fryer to 130°C (260°F). Once hot, bake the cake for 2 hours. Leave to cool in the tin.

500 g (1 lb 2 oz/2¾ cups) mixed dried fruit
zest and juice of 1 orange
75 ml (2½ fl oz/5 tablespoons) Earl Grey tea
150 g (5½ oz) soft unsalted butter, plus a little extra for greasing
150 g (5½ oz/generous ¾ cup) dark brown sugar
2 large eggs
125 g (4½ oz/1 cup) plain (all-purpose) flour
½ teaspoon baking powder
1 teaspoon mixed spice
½ teaspoon ground cinnamon
50 g (1¾ oz/½ cup) flaked (slivered) almonds
50 g (1¾ oz/¼ cup) glacé (candied) cherries, quartered

# Madeira Cake

This is the perfect weekday snacking cake – modest in appearance but effortlessly show-off in flavour.

/ Cuts into 10 /

Grease a 900 g (2 lb) loaf tin (pan) and line with baking parchment.

Add the butter and sugar to a large bowl and beat together until light and fluffy. Beat in the eggs, one by one. If the mixture begins to look curdled, then add a spoonful of the measured-out flour with the egg. Once the eggs are beaten in, add the vanilla, lemon zest and juice and milk, then beat in the flour and ground almonds. Spoon the batter into the prepared tin and smooth the top.

Heat the air fryer to 150°C (300°F). Once hot, bake the cake for 1 hour–1 hour 10 minutes until a skewer inserted into the middle comes out clean. Remove from the air fryer and leave to cool in the tin for 5 minutes before turning out onto a wire rack and leaving to cool completely.

175 g (6 oz) unsalted butter, softened, or baking spread
175 g (6 oz/¾ cup) caster (superfine) sugar
3 eggs
175 g (6 oz/scant 1½ cups) self-raising (self-rising) flour
1 teaspoon vanilla extract
zest and juice of ½ lemon
2 tablespoons milk
75 g (2½ oz/¾ cup) ground almonds

# Classic Lemon Drizzle Cake

Everyone needs a good lemon drizzle up their sleeve, and this one-bowl version couldn't be simpler to make.

/ **Cuts into 10** /

Grease a 900 g (2 lb) loaf tin (pan) and line with baking parchment.

Add the butter and sugar to a large bowl and beat together until light and fluffy. Add the eggs, one at a time, followed by the lemon juice and zest. Fold in the flour, then spoon the batter into the prepared loaf tin.

Heat the air fryer to 160°C (325°F). Once hot, bake for 50 minutes, or until risen, golden and a skewer inserted into the middle comes out clean. Remove the tin from the air fryer and poke holes all over the top with a cocktail stick (toothpick) or skewer.

Mix the topping ingredients together in a small bowl, then pour over the cake and leave to cool completely.

175 g (6 oz) unsalted butter, softened, or baking spread
175 g (6 oz/¾ cup) caster (superfine) sugar
3 eggs
zest and juice of 1 lemon
175 g (6 oz/scant 1½ cups) self-raising (self-rising) flour

FOR THE TOPPING
juice of 2 lemons
100 g (3½ oz/scant ½ cup) caster (superfine) sugar

# Banoffee Banana Bread

I've tried to elevate the usual banana bread here with a really spectacular and super-easy toffee sauce, plus some little fudgy bits in the cake as an extra sugary bonus.

/ Cuts into 10 /

Grease a 900 g (2 lb) loaf tin (pan) and line with baking parchment.

Add the butter and sugar to a large bowl and beat until it comes together and looks fluffy. Beat in the eggs, one by one, then add the vanilla and bananas and beat for 30 seconds to bring it all together. It will look a bit curdled, but don't worry the flour will fix this. Fold in the flour, baking powder and all but a small handful of the fudge and spoon into the prepared loaf tin, then sprinkle with the rest of the fudge.

Heat the air fryer to 160°C (325°F). Once hot, bake the cake for 1 hour 15 minutes, or until a skewer or cocktail stick (toothpick) inserted into the centre comes out clean. Remove from the air fryer and leave to cool in the tin for 5 minutes, then turn out onto a wire rack to cool completely.

Once cooled, melt the toffee with the double cream in a small saucepan over a low heat until runny, then pour over the top of the cooled cake before serving.

125 g (4½ oz) unsalted butter, softened, or baking spread
250 g (9 oz/scant 1 cup) caster (superfine) sugar
2 eggs
1 teaspoon vanilla extract
3–4 ripe bananas, mashed (about 350 g/12½ oz peeled weight)
250 g (9 oz/2 cups) plain (all-purpose) flour
2 teaspoons baking powder
100 g (3½ oz) fudge chunks

TO DECORATE
200 g (7 oz) toffee
6 tablespoons double (heavy) cream

# Chocolate Marble Loaf Cake

This is a fun cake to make and eat – if you have any little helpers in the kitchen, they will love swirling the batters together.

/ Cuts into 10 /

Grease a 900 g (2 lb) loaf tin (pan) and line with baking parchment.

Add the butter, sugar, flour, eggs and baking powder to a food processor and whizz until smooth. Scoop out about half of the batter into a large bowl and stir in the vanilla. Add the cocoa and milk to the remaining batter in the processor and whizz until the cocoa is fully mixed in.

Using a small spoon, blob alternating colours of the batters into the prepared tin, then using a skewer or a knife, briefly swirl the batters together, just enough so that the batters swirl into each other.

Heat the air fryer to 160°C (325°F). Once hot, place the tin in the drawer and bake for 50 minutes, or until a skewer inserted into the middle comes out clean. Remove from the air fryer and leave to cool in the tin for 5 minutes, before removing and cooling completely on a wire rack.

200 g (7 oz) unsalted butter, softened, or baking spread
200 g (7 oz/generous ¾ cup) caster (superfine) sugar
200 g (7 oz/1⅓ cups) self-raising (self-rising) flour
3 eggs
1 teaspoon baking powder
2 teaspoons vanilla extract
2 tablespoons cocoa (unsweetened cocoa) powder
1 tablespoon milk

# Rich Chocolate Cake

This rich cake is a hit with both my chocolate-obsessed son and the friends I volunteer with at the local food bank, who have declared it as a better texture than any other chocolate cake they've eaten (and they should know as they've tasted almost all the bakes from this book)!

/ Cuts into 10 /

Grease a 900 g (2 lb) loaf tin (pan) and line with baking parchment.

In a tin, over a low heat, melt together the butter and chocolate, stirring all the time. Once fully melted, set aside for about 5 minutes to cool slightly.

While the chocolate and butter mixture cools put the dry ingredients into a large mixing bowl, and stir together well, so there are no lumps and it all looks the same colour.

Stir the yoghurt into the chocolate and butter mixture. Beat together the eggs with a fork, then beat into the chocolate mixture. Make a well in the middle of the dry ingredients and pour in the chocolate mixture, then stir well until there are no lumps. Pour into the prepared loaf tin. Preheat the air fryer to 160°C (325°F) and bake for 55 minutes to 1 hour, or until a skewer comes out clean.

Once cool make up the topping. Put the chopped chocolate or chocolate chips into a heat proof bowl. Heat the cream in a saucepan until it is bubbling at the edges of the pan and the cream feels warm to touch, then pour onto the chocolate, cover and leave for a minute before stirring. Cool for 10 minutes, until the mixture is thickened (so that it doesn't just run off the cake) then spoon over the cake and swirl to cover.

175 g (6 oz) unsalted butter
100 g (3½ oz) dark chocolate, chopped
175 g (6 oz/scant 1 cup) soft light brown sugar
175 g (6 oz/1½ cups) self-raising (self-rising) flour
25 g (1 oz/¼ cup) cocoa (unsweetened cocoa) powder
½ teaspoon bicarbonate of soda (baking soda)
100 g (3½ oz) natural (plain) yoghurt
3 eggs

FOR THE TOPPING
100 g (3½ oz) chocolate, chopped
100 ml (3½ fl oz/scant ½ cup) double (heavy) cream

# Ginger Cake

This is probably my favourite cake in the whole book. It has a real ginger hit and unusually is a cake that is better the next day, as the flavour develops and the topping becomes deliciously sticky overnight.

/ Cuts into 10 /

Grease a 900 g (2 lb) loaf tin (pan) and line with baking parchment.

Add the golden syrup, sugar and butter to a small saucepan and melt over a low heat for about 5 minutes, stirring constantly until everything is well mixed and the sugar has almost all melted. At this point the mixture will be quite thick and look like caramel. Set aside to cool while you prepare the rest of the ingredients.

Add the milk and egg to a medium bowl and beat together. Stir into the cooled golden syrup mixture along with the chopped stem ginger. Mix the flour, spices and bicarbonate of soda together in a large bowl. Gradually pour the golden syrup mixture into the dry ingredients, stirring well until it is all completely mixed, then pour into the prepared tin.

Preheat the air fryer to 130°C (260°F). Once hot, bake for 50 minutes, or until a skewer inserted into the middle comes out clean. The cake should look dark brown and crusty on the outside. Remove from the air fryer and leave to cool in the tin overnight, if you can, for an extra sticky cake!

100 g (3½ oz/¼ cup) golden (light corn) syrup
100 g (3½ oz/½ cup) Demerara sugar
100 g (3½ oz) unsalted butter
150 ml (5 fl oz/scant ⅔ cup) milk
1 egg
2 balls stem ginger, drained of syrup and finely chopped
170 g (6 oz/1⅓ cups) plain (all-purpose) flour
2 teaspoons ground ginger
2 teaspoons ground cinnamon
1 teaspoon bicarbonate of soda (baking soda)

# Barabrith

I love this Welsh tea cake; I'd never tried it until I met my Welsh husband, whose mother, luckily for me, is a very good baker. This cake is for her!

/ Serves 10 /

Add the dried fruit to a heatproof bowl and pour over the hot tea. Leave to soak overnight.

The next day, grease a 900 g (2 lb) loaf tin (pan) and line with baking parchment.

In a small saucepan, melt the butter with the marmalade. Leave to cool for 5 minutes, then beat in the egg.

Add all the dry ingredients to a large bowl, stirring everything together and making sure there are no lumps of sugar. Make a well in the centre of the dry ingredients and pour in the butter mixture, the soaked fruit and any liquid left in the bowl. Stir together well, then spoon into the prepared tin.

Heat the air fryer to 140°C (275°F). Once hot, bake for 1 hour 15 minutes. Remove from the air fryer and leave to cool in the tin.

300 g (10½ oz/1⅔ cups) mixed dried fruit
250 ml (8 fl oz/1 cup) hot strong black tea
50 g (1¾ oz) unsalted butter
2 tablespoons marmalade
1 egg
300 g (10½ oz/scant 2½ cups) self-raising (self-rising) flour
100 g (3½ oz/½ cup) dark brown sugar
2 teaspoons mixed spice

# Breakfast Muffins

These muffins are vegan and a great breakfast if you're on the go. Despite the name, it would be a mistake to limit them to breakfast time – they are just as good in the afternoon with a cup of tea.

## / Makes 6 /

Line six mini pudding basins or similar with muffin cases.

Add all the dry ingredients to a large bowl and stir together to mix. In a separate bowl, mash the bananas until well squashed (if they are a bit hard then give them a quick whizz with a hand-held blender). Stir in the oil and yoghurt. Add the wet mix to the dry ingredients and mix quickly. Try not to overmix as this will make the muffins tough.

Heat the air fryer to 160°C (325°F). Once hot, divide the batter evenly between the prepared muffin cases and bake in the air fryer for 25 minutes.

150 g (5½ oz/1¼ cups) plain (all-purpose) flour
2 teaspoons baking powder
50 g (1¾ oz/¼ cup) dark brown or muscovado sugar
30 g (1 oz/⅓ cup) rolled oats, plus extra to sprinkle
50 g (1¾ oz) dried fruit (I used a mix of papaya, pineapple, raisins and apricots)
2 ripe bananas, about 300 g (10½ oz) unpeeled weight
4 tablespoons vegetable oil
100 g (3½ oz) vegan plain yoghurt

# COOKIES AND DESSERTS

# Classic Choc Chip Cookies

I've found that the best method for cooking biscuits and cookies in the air fryer is to remove the rack and bake them on a piece of baking parchment placed on the base of the air fryer basket. You can bake them in batches, or do what I often do, which is to keep the cookie dough balls in the refrigerator for up to five days, so I can have them warm from the air fryer on demand.

/ Makes 16 /

Add the butter to a large bowl and beat until soft, then add both sugars and cream together until light and fluffy. Beat in the egg, then add the flour, bicarbonate of soda and salt and beat together. When the mixture resembles breadcrumbs, add the chocolate chips, then bring the mixture together with your hands. Roll into 16 balls, about the size of golf balls and press them down lightly with your palm to form a thick disc.

Heat the air fryer to 160°C (325°F). Once hot, carefully place a sheet of baking parchment, cut to fit your air fryer, onto the base of the basket (remove the rack) and add the cookies in batches. You will need to leave space around them to expand slightly, so how many you add will depend on your air fryer. I put five in mine. Bake for 10–12 minutes, then leave in the air fryer for 10 minutes, or until the cookies are firm and can be picked up (take care as the molten chocolate may still be hot!) Transfer to a wire rack and leave to cool completely.

100 g (3½ oz) unsalted butter
100 g (3½ oz/⅓ cup) light brown soft sugar
100 g (3½ oz/scant ½ cup) caster (superfine) sugar
1 egg
300 g (10½ oz/2½ cups) self-raising (self-rising) flour
1 teaspoon bicarbonate of soda (baking soda)
pinch of salt
100 g (3½ oz/generous ½ cup) dark chocolate chips

# Chocolate 'Pizza' Cookie

These are great for picnics and parties, but even better served warm from the air fryer with a scoop of vanilla ice cream as a dessert.

/ **Cuts into 8 slices per cookie** /

On a piece of baking parchment draw around the base of a 20 cm (8 in) cake tin (the base not the top, as the top is too big and your cookie will be too thin). Ideally the circle will measure 18 cm (7 in) in diameter, but no bigger. Repeat this so you have two circles. Set aside.

Add the butter and sugar to a large bowl and beat with a hand-held electric whisk until well mixed. Beat in the egg, then add the flour, cocoa and salt and beat until thoroughly combined.

Divide the batter into two and, with damp hands, press out to fill the circles you've drawn on the baking parchment. Scatter over the chocolate chunks then press into the dough. Leave to chill in the refrigerator for 30–60 minutes to firm up.

Once the cookie is firm, trim the baking parchment 2 cm (1 in) from the edge of the pizza cookies so they have space to expand, but also so that there isn't too much parchment flapping around in the air fryer, which can hamper the baking of the cookie and make it a funny shape.

Heat the air fryer to 160°C (325°F) Once hot, transfer the cookie to the air fryer (on to the rack) still on the baking parchment and bake for 15 minutes. Open the air fryer and leave the cookie for a few minutes, until it is solid enough to move it then, cut into wedges like a pizza while still warm. Repeat with the second piece of dough. Leave to cool until firm.

80 g (3 oz) unsalted butter
150 g (5 oz/1 cup) light brown soft sugar
1 egg
160 g (6 oz/1½ cup) self-raising (self-rising) flour
2 tablespoon cocoa (unsweetened cocoa) powder
¼ teaspoon salt
30 g (11/4 oz) white chocolate, cut into chunks
30 g (1¼ oz) dark chocolate, cut into chunks

# Shortbread Petticoat Tails

According to the Walkers, the famous Scottish shortbread makers, petticoat tails get their name because they look like fabric used to create elaborate petticoats in the 12th century. However they got their name, this is a really easy way of baking shortbread, which in its uncooked form can be super crumbly. This way the crumbs are encased in the tin and bake together to form a delicious melt-in-the-mouth cookie.

/ Cuts into 8–10 /

Grease a 20 cm (8 in) fluted, loose-bottomed tart tin and line the base with baking parchment (a little greasing of butter on the base will stick the parchment down).

Whizz the butter and sugar in a food processor until smooth, then add the flours and whizz until the mixture looks like large breadcrumbs. Tip this mixture into the prepared tin, then using the back of a spoon, press down evenly until the top is flat. Place in the refrigerator to chill for at least 1 hour.

Once the shortbread is chilled and firm, prick all over with a fork. Heat the air fryer to 130°C (266°F). Once hot, transfer the shortbread, still in the tin, to the air fryer and bake for 30–40 minutes. While the shortbread is still hot, cut it into 8–10 petticoat tails and leave to cool in the tin.

100 g (3½ oz) cold salted butter, plus extra for greasing

50 g (1¾ oz/scant ¼ cup) caster (superfine) sugar, plus extra 2 teaspoons for sprinkling

150 g (5½ oz/1¼ cups) plain (all-purpose) flour

25 g (¾ oz/3 tablespoons) rice flour

# Coconut Macaroons

My grandma used to make these all the time when I was a kid. When I decided these would be a great recipe for the air fryer, I couldn't work out how she had shaped them into perfect cones, but then out of the recesses of my mind it came to me and I remembered the egg cup! Grandma's were a bit more pointed than my version, but the shape all depends on your own egg cup.

/ Makes about 14 /

Add the egg whites and sugar to a large bowl and beat with a hand-held electric whisk for a few minutes until the sugar has dissolved and the mixture is thick. Add the cornflour and beat in for a minute, then add the coconut and stir everything together well.

Spoon the mixture into an egg cup, then turn out onto a piece of baking parchment or reusable liner. I bake four at a time as that seems to ensure even baking.

Heat the air fryer to 150°C (300°F). Once hot, bake the macaroons in batches for 10–12 minutes until lightly golden and set. Leave to cool completely on the baking parchment, then dip the base of the macaroons into the melted chocolate and arrange on baking parchment to set.

2 egg whites
100 g (3½ oz/scant ½ cup) caster (superfine) sugar
1 teaspoon cornflour (cornstarch)
200 g (7 oz/scant 2¼ cups) desiccated (dried shredded) coconut
100 g (3½ oz) dark chocolate, melted

# Vegan Thumb Print Cookies

A simple, fun family favourite, but plant-based. You could replace the jam with a vegan chocolate spread or even peanut butter, if you like.

/ Makes 9 /

Add all the ingredients, except for the jam, to a small bowl, and using your fingertips, rub in the butter. Once the butter is well rubbed in, bring it together to form a dough. Cover the dough with cling film (plastic wrap) and leave to chill in the refrigerator for 30 minutes.

Once the dough is chilled and firm, divide it into nine pieces and roll into balls.

Heat the air fryer to 150°C (300°F). Once hot, press a thumb or finger into the middle of each ball, then arrange the cookies on a piece of baking parchment on the rack in the air fryer and spoon some jam into each indentation. Bake for 10–15 minutes until firm and turning slightly golden.

50 g (1¾ oz) cold plant-based butter, cut into cubes
1 tablespoon icing (powdered) sugar
50 g (1¾ oz/scant ½ cup) plain (all-purpose) flour
50 g (1¾ oz/½ cup) ground almonds
pinch of salt
about 5 teaspoons jam

# Pecan and Ginger Shortbread

I have based this shortbread on my favourite Christmas biscuits (cookies) from Fortnum and Mason that are only available during the festive season. They've turned out to be a pretty good alternative, so now I can have them at any time of the year! I tend to make a batch, bake half, then put the rest in the freezer for a treat another time. If you want to do that too, then these can be sliced, frozen as discs and baked straight from frozen.

**/ Makes 22 /**

Whizz the butter, sugar and salt together in a food processor to a smooth paste. Add the flours and whizz until it all comes together. Turn out onto a work surface and knead in the pecans and ginger. Using a sheet of baking parchment or cling film (plastic wrap), roll into a log, about 25 cm (10 in) long and leave to chill in the refrigerator for at least 1 hour, or until firm.

Once chilled, unroll the log and slice into 1 cm (½ in) thick cookies.

Heat the air fryer to 160°C (325°F) and cut a piece of baking parchment to fit the base. Once hot, place the parchment in the air fryer and transfer the cookies in batches to bake for 10 minutes. These don't spread too much, so you should be able to fit a few in at once. Once they are baked, leave in the air fryer for a few minutes until the cookies have set and can be removed. Transfer to a wire rack and leave to cool completely.

The shortbread dough log will keep in the refrigerator for a week and cookies can be sliced off as and when you like if you don't want to eat them all at once. Alternatively, the cut cookies can be frozen and cooked straight from the freezer. Depending on your air fryer, they may need 1–2 minutes more cooking from frozen.

150 g (5½ oz) cold unsalted butter
75 g (2½ oz/⅔ cup) caster (superfine) sugar
pinch of salt
175 g (6 oz/scant 1½ cups) plain (all-purpose) flour
50 g (1¾ oz/generous ¼ cup) rice flour
25 g (¾ oz/¼ cup) pecan nuts, chopped
25 g (¾ oz) crystallised (candied) ginger, chopped

# Pistachio and White Chocolate Biscotti

These twice-baked biscuits are so quick and easy to make. I don't like my biscotti to be too hard, so I tend to only bake them for 5 minutes on the second bake after slicing, but if you want them to be really crisp leave them in for 10. I love the combination of pistachio and white chocolate but any chocolate and nut combination you like will work just as well.

/ Makes 20 /

Chop about a third of the pistachios finely. With hand-held electric whisk, beat together the egg and sugar until the mix is thick and creamy, then fold in the flour, bicarbonate of soda and the chopped and whole pistachio nuts. The dough will be soft.

Turn out onto a lightly floured work surface and shape into a 20 cm (8 in) long, flat sausage about 1.5 cm (¾ in) thick and 6 cm (3 in) wide.

Heat the air fryer to 160°C (325°F). Once hot, place the dough into the air fryer rack on a piece of baking parchment and bake for 20 mins, then turn over and bake for 10 minutes.

Take out of the air fryer and cut into 1 cm thick slices with a small serrated knife, while still warm. Heat the air fryer again to 140°C (275°F) and once hot, bake the slices in batches for 5–10 minutes until crisp. Cool on a wire rack, then dip into melted chocolate to coat half the biscuits. Leave to set on baking parchment.

30 g (1 oz) pistachios
1 egg
50 g (1¾ oz) caster (superfine) sugar
125 g (5 oz) plain ( all-purpose) flour
¼ tsp bicarbonate of soda (baking soda)
100 g (3½ oz) white chocolate, melted for dipping

# Oat Cookies

This recipe makes quite a lot of cookies, so if you feel you can't eat that many, then they can be frozen as squashed balls and baked straight from the freezer, but you'll need to add another couple of minutes to the bake time.

## / Makes 20 /

Add the butter and sugar to a large bowl and beat together until light and fluffy. Beat in the egg and vanilla, followed by the flour, baking powder and salt. Finally, stir in the oats. Roll the mixture into 20 balls, a little smaller than a golf ball.

Heat the air fryer to 150°C (300°F). Once hot, carefully place a sheet of baking parchment, cut to fit your air fryer, onto the base of the basket (remove the rack) and add the cookies in batches. You will need to leave space around them to expand slightly, so how many you add will depend on your air fryer. I put six in mine. Press to flatten slightly and bake for 15 minutes.

Leave to cool for 5 minutes in the air fryer until the cookies are firm enough to move to a wire rack to cool completely.

125 g (4½ oz) soft unsalted butter
200 g (7 oz/1 cup) soft brown sugar
1 egg
1 teaspoon vanilla extract
125 g (4½ oz/1 cup) plain (all-purpose) flour
1 teaspoon baking powder
pinch of salt
200 g (7 oz/2 cups) rolled oats

# Meringue Nests

I prefer to use white caster (superfine) sugar to make meringues, not for the colour but because often golden caster sugar isn't quite as fine as white. If the sugar isn't fully melted into the meringue mixture when you bake them it tends to weep out of the meringues at the bottom. It's not a big problem, but it you want your meringues to be as perfect as possible then go for white caster sugar! This recipe can be halved to make two nests if you have a smaller air fryer.

/ Makes 4 /

Using a hand-held electric whisk, beat the eggs in a large bowl until thick and frothy, then gradually add the sugar, beating well after each addition. Add the vinegar with the last batch of sugar. Once all the sugar is added keep beating for a few more minutes. This is to try to dissolve all the sugar as much as possible. The mixture should be stiff and very glossy.

Heat the air fryer to 100°C (210°F). Once hot, cut a piece of baking parchment to the size of the base of your air fryer and dot one side with a few blobs of the meringue mixture and press this, blob-side down onto the base of the air fryer. This will attach the parchment to the base of the air fryer, which will make it easier for you to spoon over the meringue, but should also prevent the parchment from flying about once the air fryer is turned on. Spoon four large blobs onto the parchment and make hollows in the middle of each. The meringues will puff up slightly so make sure there is some space between them. Close the drawer of the air fryer and bake for 1 hour 30 minutes. Leave the meringues in the air fryer overnight if you can. They should be crisp on the outside and marshmallowy in the middle. Serve with whipped cream and fruit.

2 egg whites
100 g (3½ oz/scant ½ cup) caster (superfine) sugar
½ teaspoon white wine vinegar

TO SERVE
whipped cream
fresh fruit of choice

# Classic Pavlova

My mum is a brilliant cook and growing up her go-to dessert for parties was always a huge delicious lemon cream pavlova. This air fryer pav is smaller and a little more traditional, but I think she'll still approve.

/ Serves 8–10 /

Using a hand-held whisk, whisk the egg whites in a large bowl until frothy. With the beaters mixing, beat in the sugar, 1 tablespoon at a time, adding the vinegar and cornflour with the last spoonful of sugar. Continue to beat for another 3–4 minutes until thick and glossy.

Cut a piece of baking parchment to a 22 cm (8½ in) diameter circle, or whatever size will fit into the base of your air fryer. Dot a little of the meringue mixture onto one side of the parchment and press this, blob-side down into the air fryer. This will attach the parchment to the base of the air fryer, which will make it easier for you to spoon over the meringue, but should also prevent the parchment from flying about once turned on.

Spoon in a few spoonfuls of the meringue onto the baking parchment and spread to almost the edge of your parchment, to create a base for the pavlova, then add spoonfuls all around the edge of the circle, almost creating a wall all the way around. Heat the air fryer to 130°C (260°F). Close the drawer and bake for 15 minutes. Then, turn the air fryer down to 110°C (225°F) and cook for another 45 minutes. Leave in the air fryer overnight if you can, or for at least 2 hours.

Leave the frozen fruits to defrost on a plate, then pop 200 g (7 oz) of them into a medium saucepan with the sugar. Bring to the boil, then simmer for 3 minutes. Remove from the heat and purée with a hand-held blender, then strain into a jug to remove any seeds and skins. You should have about 100 ml (3½ fl oz/scant ½ cup) of sauce. If there is any juice from the rest of the fruit, this can also be added to the sauce. Leave to cool.

Beat the cream until thick, then spoon into the the pavlova. Top with the fruit and drizzle over a little of the sauce and serving the rest in a jug alongside.

3 egg whites
150 g (5½ oz/⅔ cup) caster (superfine) sugar
½ teaspoon white wine vinegar
½ teaspoon cornflour (cornstarch)

FOR THE TOP
500 g (1 lb 2 oz) frozen summer berries
100 g (3½ oz/scant ½ cup) caster (superfine) sugar
300 ml (10 fl oz/1¼ cups) double (heavy) cream

# Brownies

This recipe had a few iterations, before I decided that this was 'the one'. For me, a brownie should be like a cake, but fudgy in the middle and should not be so soft that they require setting in the refrigerator before you can cut and eat them! Sadly the air fryer can't produce the perfect brownie, but my family thought these were pretty awesome.

/ Cuts into 16 /

Grease and line the base of a 20 cm (8 in) square cake tin (pan) with baking parchment.

Melt the butter and chocolate together in a small saucepan over a very low heat, stirring until completely melted. Remove from the heat and set aside.

In a large bowl, whisk the eggs and sugar together with a hand-held electric whisk for about 3 minutes, or until pale, thickened and frothy, then gently pour in the melted chocolate and butter mixture. sift in the flour, cocoa and salt and gently fold everything together until combined. Pour the batter into the prepared tin.

Heat the air fryer to 160°C (325°F). Once hot, bake the brownies for 25–30 minutes. The brownie should be soft, but not runny. Leave to cool in the tin before cutting.

125 g (4½ oz) unsalted butter, plus extra for greasing
125 g (4½ oz) dark chocolate, chopped into small pieces
2 eggs
150 g (5½ oz/⅔ cup) caster (superfine) sugar
50 g (1¾ oz/scant ½ cup) plain (all-purpose) flour
30 g (1¾ oz/¼ cup) cocoa (unsweetened cocoa) powder
pinch of salt

# Malted Milk Blondies

Blondies are my favourite and I've been making a version of these malted milk ones in my fan oven for a few years now. I'm so pleased to have perfected the recipe for my air fryer too!

/ Cuts into 12–16 /

Grease and line the base of a 20 cm (8 in) square cake tin (pan) with baking parchment.

Add the butter to a small saucepan and gently melt over a medium heat. Remove from the heat and leave to cool down slightly.

Add the eggs and sugar to a large bowl and whisk together with a hand-held whisk for a few minutes, or until thick and frothy. Whisk through the melted butter and vanilla, then finally, fold in the flour, malted milk powder and baking powder. Gently pour into the prepared tin and scatter over the chocolate.

Heat the air fryer to 160°C (325°F). Once hot, transfer the tin to the drawer and bake for 30 minutes. They are done when a skewer inserted into the centre comes out with sticky crumbs but isn't wet. Leave to cool completely in the tin. Cut into 12–16 squares and store in a cake tin or airtight container for up to three days.

125 g (4½ oz) salted butter, plus extra for greasing
2 eggs
150 g (5½ oz/generous ¾ cup) soft brown sugar
1 teaspoon vanilla extract
125 g (4½ oz/1 cup) plain (all-purpose) flour
3 tablespoons malted milk powder
½ teaspoon baking powder
50 g (1¾ oz) dark chocolate, cut into chunks

# Rhubarb Crumble Slice

Is this a biscuit or is this a dessert? I'm not sure, but whatever it is, it is delicious! The leftover syrup from the rhubarb is fantastic drizzled over vanilla ice cream, or stirred into cocktails, so don't discard it.

/ Cuts into about 20 /

Put the rhubarb and sugar into a small saucepan and cook over a low heat for about 10 minutes, until the rhubarb is soft. Drain the rhubarb through a sieve into a jug, keeping the pink syrup that is created. Set aside.

In a food processor, whizz the butter, flour, sugar and a pinch of salt until the mixture looks like chunky breadcrumbs and is just starting to clump together. Line a 20 cm (8 in) square cake tin (pan) with foil and press about two-thirds of the crumble mixture into the base, levelling with the back of a spoon.

Heat the air fryer to 160°C (325°F) and bake for 20 minutes, until golden and looking crisp.

Once the base is baked, spread the prepared rhubarb over the top, then sprinkle on the remaining crumble topping. Return to the air fryer and bake for 15 minutes, until the top is golden. Leave to cool.

Once cool, in a small bowl, mix the icing sugar with 1 tablespoon of the rhubarb syrup and drizzle this over the crumble before cutting into squares.

500 g (1 lb 2 oz) rhubarb, chopped into 2 cm (¾ in) chunks
100 g (3½ oz/1 scant cup) caster (superfine) sugar
200 g (8 oz) cold unsalted butter, cut into small chunks
275 g (9¾ oz/2¼ cups) plain (all-purpose) flour
125 g (5 oz/⅔ cup) light brown soft sugar
pinch of salt
3 tablespoons icing (powdered) sugar

# Chocolate Puddle Cakes

This is a brilliant dessert for the air fryer, as the little pots need hardly any cooking time. They can also be made a day ahead and kept in the refrigerator until you're almost ready to eat them, then just bake them in the air fryer for 12 minutes, and your speedy pudding is ready!

/ Makes 4 /

Add 25 g (¾ oz) of the butter to a microwave-safe bowl and heat in the microwave for 20 seconds. You need the butter to be softly spreadable, rather than completely runny. Using a brush, grease four mini pudding basins thickly with the melted butter, then dust with the cocoa. Make sure the butter is covered completely with the cocoa, as this will stop the cakes sticking to the moulds.

Add the remaining butter and the chocolate to a small tin and melt together over the lowest heat, stirring constantly. Remove from the heat and set aside.

Using a hand-held electric whisk, beat the whole eggs, egg yolks and the sugar together in a large bowl for 5 minutes, or until the mixture has become pale and fluffy and doubled in volume. When you lift the beaters from the mixture it should briefly leave a trail behind on the surface. Pour in the melted butter and chocolate mixture and whisk in, then sift in the flour and fold this in completely. Divide the mixture between the prepared moulds.

Heat the air fryer to 160°C (325°F). Once hot, bake the cakes for 12 minutes. The cakes will be well risen above the top of their moulds. Remove them from the air fryer with oven gloves and turn out onto plates to serve. These are great served with some thick cream or crème fraîche.

125 g (4½ oz) unsalted butter
about 2 teaspoons cocoa (unsweetened cocoa) powder, for dusting
150 g (5½ oz) dark chocolate
2 large eggs
2 large egg yolks
55 g (2 oz/scant ¼ cup) caster (superfine) sugar
35 g (1¾ oz/generous ¼ cup) plain (all-purpose) flour
thick cream or crème fraîche, to serve

# Sweet Cherry Scones

Scones are such a great thing to make; super easy, really quick and family and friends are always impressed with homemade scones. Imagine how impressed they'll be when you tell them you made them in your air fryer! I love these with dried cherries, but you can use any dried fruit you like.

/ Makes 8 /

Add the flour, baking powder, sugar, salt and dried fruit to a large bowl, then add the butter and rub it in with your fingertips until there are no lumps and it resembles breadcrumbs. Add the buttermilk and cut it in with a knife until it makes a raggedy looking dough, then bring the dough together with your hands.

Turn the dough out onto a lightly floured work surface and pat the dough into a round, about 1.5 cm (⅝ in) thick. Using a 6 cm (2½ in) cutter, cut out rounds. Bring the remaining dough together again and cut out more rounds until you have used up all the dough.

Heat the air fryer to 180°C (350°F). Once hot, bake the scones for 10 minutes, or until lightly golden. Sprinkle with the extra sugar as soon as they are out of the air fryer.

225 g (8 oz/generous 1¾ cups) self-raising (self-rising) flour, plus extra for dusting
½ teaspoon baking powder
25 g (¾ oz/1 heaped tablespoon) caster (superfine) sugar, plus extra for sprinkling
pinch of salt
50 g (1¾ oz) dried cherries
50 g (1¾ oz) unsalted butter
125 g (4½ oz) buttermilk or plain yoghurt

# Baked Lemon Cheesecake

My husband said this is the best cheesecake I've ever made – and believe me, I've written a lot of cheesecake recipes. I couldn't believe how well this recipe turned out considering how tricky a baked cheesecake can be. It may split on cooling, but that can be hidden with the lemon curd if it you like a neater finish.

/ Serves 10 /

Line the base of a 20 cm (8 in) springform cake tin (pan).

Whizz the biscuits in a food processor until crumbs, or add to a sandwich bag, seal the top and bash with a rolling pin until they are crumbs. Transfer the crumbs to a bowl and stir in the melted butter, then press into the prepared tin.

Heat the air fryer to 160°C (325°F). Once hot, bake the base for 5 minutes.

Clean the food processor (if used), then add the cream cheese, sugar, crème fraiche, eggs, flour and lemon zest and juice and whizz together until smooth. Pour this on top of the baked base. Cover with kitchen foil and bake for 30 minutes, then remove the foil and bake for another 30–35 minutes. The edges will be firm but the middle will have a slight wobble.

Leave to cool completely before removing from the tin and spreading over the lemon curd.

10 digestive biscuits (graham crackers)

50 g (1¾ oz) unsalted butter, melted

600 g (1 lb 5 oz/scant 2½ cups) full-fat cream cheese

200 g (7 oz/generous ¾ cup) caster (superfine) sugar

150 ml (5 fl oz/scant ⅔ cup) crème fraîche

3 eggs

2 tablespoons plain (all-purpose) flour

zest and juice of 1 lemon

5 tablespoons lemon curd

# Choux Pastry

At the weekend I love to have a cream cake, and the king of the cream cake, for me, is the éclair, though I'll happily take a profiterole if éclairs aren't available. These are a cinch to make in the air fryer, although they must be cooked in batches. This choux recipe makes both éclairs and profiteroles, so choose which ones you prefer. I know what I'll be making...

/ Makes about 18–20 profiteroles and 8–10 éclairs /

Sift the flour onto a large piece of baking parchment. Add the milk, butter, sugar, salt and water to a small saucepan and heat over a medium heat until the butter is melted. Increase the heat and once the liquid is boiling, using the baking parchment as a chute, quickly pour the flour into the pan. Beat well until the mixture is smooth, then remove from the heat and leave to stand for about 15 minutes, or until it is just about room temperature.

Once cooled slightly, using a wooden spoon or silicone spatula, beat the eggs, one by one into the mixture in the pan.

FOR THE CHOUX PASTRY
85 g (3 oz/generous ⅔ cup) plain (all-purpose) flour
75 g (2½ oz/5 tablespoons) whole milk
60 g (2 oz) butter
1½ teaspoons caster (superfine) sugar
pinch of salt
75 g (2½ oz/5 tablespoons) water
2 eggs

## TO MAKE SALTED CARAMEL AND CHOCOLATE ÉCLAIRS:

Fit a 1.5 cm (⅝ in) round nozzle on a piping bag and spoon in the choux. Cut a piece of baking parchment to fit your air fryer and pipe out lines of the mixture about 10–12 cm (4–4½ in) long and 5 cm (2 in) apart. I can fit four at a time in my air fryer. I like to draw a line on the back of the baking parchment, so I have a size to follow when I'm piping my choux. Heat the air fryer to 160°C (325°F). Once hot, bake for 20–25 minutes. Remove the éclairs from the air fryer, turn them over and, using a skewer, poke a hole in the base of each to let any steam escape. Return to the air fryer upside down and bake for another 5 minutes until crisp all over.

To make the topping, put the cream into a small saucepan over a low heat and bring just to the boil (little bubbles will appear around the edge). Put the chocolate chips into a heatproof bowl and pour over the just boiling cream. Cover and leave to stand for 2–3 minutes then add the butter and stir until smooth and glossy.

For the filling, whip the cream with a hand-held electric whisk until just holding it's shape then spoon into a piping bag fitted with a star nozzle.

To assemble, split the cooled éclairs lengthways. Spread about 1 teaspoon of the salted caramel into the base of the éclair, then pipe over the cream. Finally dip the top of the pastry into the chocolate, to just cover, then pop on top of the cream filling. Leave in a cool place (but not the refrigerator) until the chocolate has just set before serving. These are best served the day they are made, but will keep overnight in the refrigerator, though the pastry will not be as crisp.

FOR THE ÉCLAIR FILLING
300 ml (10 fl oz/1¼ cup) double (heavy) cream
1 tablespoon icing (powdered) sugar
50-75 g (2–3 oz) salted caramel sauce

FOR THE ÉCLAIR TOPPING
50 ml (1¾ fl oz/¼ cup) double (heavy) cream
50 g (2 oz) dark chocolate chips
10 g (½ oz) unsalted butter

## TO MAKE PEANUT BUTTER AND JAM (JELLY) PROFITEROLES:

Spoon the choux into a piping bag fitted with a large round nozzle. Cut a piece of baking parchment to fit your air fryer and pipe out rounds of mixture a little smaller than a golf ball, spaced about 3 cm (1¼ in) apart. I can fit nine at a time in my air fryer, so I usually do these in three batches. Heat the air fryer to 160°C (325°F). Once hot, bake for 20–25 minutes until they are puffed up and golden. Remove from the air fryer, turn the balls over and, using a skewer, poke a hole in the base of each to let any steam escape. Return to the air fryer upside down and bake for another 5 minutes until crisp all over.

To make the topping put the jam into a small saucepan and heat over a low heat until it is runny, sieve this if there are seeds or lumps of raspberry to make a smooth jam. Stir this into the icing sugar to make a pink sauce. Set aside.

For the filling beat the cream with a hand-held electric whisk with the peanut butter and icing sugar, until it is just holding its shape. Spoon into a piping bag fitted with a star nozzle.

Split the cooled profiteroles horizontally. Pipe the cream into the base of each bun. Dip the tops into the raspberry sauce, then pop them on top of the cream filling. Leave in a cool place (but not the refrigerator) until the raspberry topping has just set before serving. These are best served he day they are made, but will keep overnight in the refrigerator, though the pastry will not be as crisp.

FOR THE PROFITEROLE FILLING
300 ml (12 fl oz/21/4 cup) double (heavy) cream
75 g (3 oz) smooth peanut butter
2 tablespoons icing (powdered) sugar

FOR THE PROFITEROLE TOPPING
4 tablespoons raspberry jam, heated and sieved
100 g (4 oz) icing (powdered) sugar

# Apricot and Raspberry Tart

How you make this tart will depend on the shape and size of your air fryer. Mine can fit a 23 cm (9 in) diameter circle of puff pastry, but if yours is not as big as mine, then make the tart either smaller or into another shape, such as a square or even a rectangle. Cooking times will stay the same. This tart is really simple and super easy to make. To save time you can bake the pastry before hand and leave it in your air fryer until you need to add the topping.

/ Serves 6–8 /

Unroll the puff pastry and use a plate to cut out a circle. My plate was 23 cm (9 in) in diameter, which fits my air fryer. Using a sharp knife, score a line around the circle, about 1 cm (½ in) in from the edge to create a lip.

Heat the air fryer to 180°C (350°F). Once hot, bake the puff pastry on a sheet of baking parchment on the rack of the air fryer for 8–10 minutes. It should be puffed and golden.

Open the air fryer and leaving the pastry inside, press it down in the middle, leaving the puffed edge. Sprinkle over the ground almonds and 1 tablespoon of the sugar, then arrange over the apricots.

Heat the air fryer to 160°C (325°F). Once hot, bake for 10 minutes. Add the raspberries, sprinkle over the remaining sugar and bake for another 15 minutes. Serve warm with thick double (heavy) cream or crème fraîche.

320 g (10¼ oz) sheet ready-rolled puff pastry
2 tablespoons ground almonds
2 tablespoons Demerara sugar
6–8 small apricots, stoned and quartered
100 g (3½ oz) raspberries
double (heavy) cream or crème fraîche, to serve

# Raspberry Bakewell Tarts

These tarts are great as an afternoon tea treat, or served as a dessert, still warm with a little thick cream. When lining the tarts with the baking paper, make sure to keep the paper quite neat, as any long bits may catch the heating element of the air fryer.

/ Makes 4 /

Roll the pastry a little wider, then cut into four squares. Press the pastry into four 10 cm (4 in) loose-bottomed tart tins (pans). Trim the edges and prick the bases a few times with a fork. Chill in the refrigerator for at least 30 minutes.

Heat the air fryer to 160°C (325°F). Once hot, line the pastry cases with baking parchment and baking beans, then bake for 10 minutes. Remove the parchment and beans and return to the air fryer for 5 minutes, or until the bases of the tarts are lightly golden and fully baked.

Beat the butter and caster sugar together in a large bowl, then beat in the ground almonds and egg. Spread 1 teaspoon of the jam into the bases of the tart cases, then divide the ground almond mixture evenly between them. Spread to level the top. Push four raspberry halves into each tart. Bake for 20 minutes, until golden and firm in the middle.

Meanwhile, mix the icing sugar with 2 tablespoons of water, then drizzle over the tarts.

200 g (7 oz) ready-rolled shortcrust pastry
50 g (1¾ oz) soft unsalted butter
50 g (1¾ oz/scant ¼ cup) caster (superfine) sugar
50 g (1¾ oz/½ cup) ground almonds
1 egg
4 teaspoons raspberry jam
8 raspberries, halved
6 tablespoons icing (powdered) sugar

# Plum and Ginger Crumble

This is such an easy crumble to make, as unlike apples and rhubarb, the plums need very little cooking before they're topped with the spiced crumble.

/ Serves 6 /

Add the plums, stem ginger and syrup and sugar to a baking dish. I used a 21 cm (8½ in) enamel dish. Stir together and cover with kitchen foil.

Heat the air fryer to 180°C (350°F). Once hot, bake the covered fruit for 15–20 minutes. This will depend on how ripe your plums are, they need to be softened before they're topped with the crumble, so check them occasionally as they bake.

Meanwhile, make the crumble. Add the butter and flour to a large bowl and, using your fingertips, rub the butter into the flour until the mixture resembles breadcrumbs. Stir in the sugar and ground ginger.

Once the fruit has had 15–20 minutes and has started to soften and become juicy, remove the kitchen foil and sprinkle over the crumble (I quite like to squash some of it together in my hand to make some chunky clumps). Bake in the air fryer for another 10–15 minutes until the crumble is golden. Serve with lashings of cream.

6 plums, stoned and quartered
1 ball stem ginger, chopped, plus 2 tablespoons syrup from the jar
2 teaspoons caster (superfine) sugar
double (heavy) cream, to serve

FOR THE CRUMBLE
60 g (2 oz) unsalted butter, cold from the refrigerator and cut into cubes
100 g (3½ oz/generous ¾ cup) plain (all-purpose) flour
25 g (¾ oz/2 tablespoons) caster (superfine) sugar
½ teaspoon ground ginger

# Brioche Bread and Butter Pudding

Brioche smothered with butter and apricot jam has been a favourite of mine ever since university, when my friend Ruth and I ate it as a treat every Sunday while watching breakfast TV. Swap the jam to another flavour, if you prefer – it'll be just as good!

## / Serves 4 /

Butter the brioche slices and spread over the jam. Arrange the brioche in a 20 cm (8 in) square ceramic dish, or whatever fits your air fryer. In a large bowl, beat the eggs, cream and milk together, then pour over the brioche and leave to soak in the refrigerator for 30–60 minutes.

Heat the air fryer to 160°C (325°F). Once hot, sprinkle the Demerara sugar over the soaked brioche and bake for 20–25 minutes until the custard is set and the brioche has crispy edges. Tuck in while it's warm with cream, if you like.

soft salted butter, for spreading
6 slices brioche
6 heaped teaspoons apricot jam
2 eggs
100 ml (3½ fl oz/scant ½ cup) double (heavy) cream
200 ml (7 fl oz/scant 1 cup) milk
1 tablespoon Demerara sugar
cream, to serve (optional)

# Tarte Tatin

I knew this French classic would work well in the air fryer because the top down heat works perfectly for the puff pastry. I like to use a crisp eating (dessert) apple like Granny Smith for this as I like the flavour and it keeps its shape well.

/ Serves 6 /

Unroll the pastry and place a 20 cm (8 in) sandwich cake tin (pan) upside down on top. Cut around the tin to create your perfectly sized piece of pastry, then set aside.

Heat the sugar in a small saucepan over a low heat until dissolved and golden brown. Add the butter and stir to create a caramel. Pour this into the base of the cake tin you drew around, then top with the apple quarters.

Heat the air fryer to 180°C (350°F). Once hot, transfer the tin to the air fryer and bake for 10 minutes.

After 10 minutes, top the apples with the pastry, pressing the sides down into the tin. Bake for another 20 minutes, until the pastry is puffed and golden. Remove from the air fryer and leave to cool slightly before placing a serving plate on top and turning it upside down. Serve warm with crème fraîche, whipped cream or ice cream.

320 g (10¼ oz) sheet ready-rolled puff pastry
75 g (2½ oz/⅓ cup) caster (superfine) sugar
75 g (3 oz) unsalted butter
4 apples, peeled, cored and cut into quarters (I used Granny Smith)
crème fraîche, whipped cream or ice cream, to serve

# Hazelnut and Chocolate Baklava-style Rolls

This is so much simpler than it looks – using ready-chopped nuts and chocolate chips saves so much time, making it a lot quicker than a traditional baklava recipe.

/ Cuts into about 18 /

Butter a 20 cm (8 in) sandwich cake tin (pan) with a little of the melted butter.

For the syrup, add the sugar, water and golden syrup to a saucepan and cook over a medium heat, stirring until the sugar has dissolved. Once dissolved, increase the heat slightly and simmer for another 5 minutes, or until syrupy. Remove from the heat and set aside.

Mix two thirds of the chocolate chips and all of the nuts together in a small bowl. Take a sheet of filo pastry and brush with the melted butter, then top with another sheet of pastry and brush with more butter. Sprinkle one-third of the chocolate chip and nut mixture in a line along one of the long sides of the buttered pastry. Spoon 2–3 tablespoons of the syrup over the chocolate and nuts, then fold the pastry over and start to roll up, brushing with butter every time you roll it over. One fully rolled, coil into a spiral and place in the prepared cake tin. Repeat this to make two more spirals. Once they are all in the tin, brush with the remaining butter.

Heat the air fryer to 160°C (325°F). Once hot, bake for 15 minutes, then brush with more of the syrup and return to the air fryer for another 10–15 minutes. Remove from the air fryer and spoon over the remaining syrup.

Melt the remaining chocolate, then drizzle over the rolls and scatter with the remaining nuts. Leave for at least 15 minutes, before cutting into pieces.

100 g (3½ oz) unsalted butter, melted
150 g (5 oz) dark chocolate chips
100 g (3½ oz/generous ¾ cup) roasted and chopped hazelnuts, plus a few extra to sprinkle
6 sheets filo pastry

FOR THE SYRUP
125 g (4½ oz/½ cup) caster (superfine) sugar
100 ml (3½ fl oz/scant ½ cup) water
2 tablespoons golden (light corn) syrup

# Little Apple Pies

These little pies, a bit like the ones from that famous burger joint, are so quick and easy to make you'll never need to buy the takeaway version again!

/ Makes 6 /

Add the apples, caster sugar and lemon juice to a large saucepan and cook for 5 minutes, stirring, until the apples are softened, but not falling apart and the liquid is juicy. Stir in the cornflour and cook for 1 minute to thicken. Remove from the heat and leave to cool.

Unroll the pastry and sprinkle over the Demerara sugar, then using a rolling pin, roll over the sugar, pressing it into the pastry. Turn the pastry over, so it is sugar-side down. This will be on the outside.

With the long side facing you, fold the pastry over itself towards you and cut into six equal pieces, along the fold. Unfold the pastry, you should have six long strips. Divide the apple mixture between one half of each piece of pastry, leaving space at the edges. Brush the uncovered side of pastry with the beaten egg, then pull that half over the top of the filling. Press down at the sides and crimp to seal with a fork. Repeat this with all the pies and brush the tops with the remaining egg.

Heat the air fryer to 180°C (350°F). Once hot, bake the pies for 5 minutes, then turn over and bake for another 4 minutes on the other side. Leave to cool on a rack for a few minutes before tucking in.

3 apples, peeled, cored and finely diced (I used Granny Smith)
50 g (1¾ oz/scant ¼ cup) caster (superfine) sugar
½ teaspoon ground cinnamon
juice of ½ lemon
1 teaspoon cornflour (cornstarch)
320 g (10¼ oz) sheet ready-rolled shortcrust pastry
4 tablespoons Demerara sugar
1 egg, beaten

# SAVOURY BAKES

# Savoury Scones

These scones are so easy to make and perfect for a picnic lunch, or even a lunch al desko. I do love this classic flavour combination, but they are also really easy to tailor to your tastes. Try swapping the spring onions for sundried tomatoes or even the Cheddar for a blue cheese, the choice is yours!

/ Makes 6 /

Mix all the dry ingredients together in a large bowl, then add the butter cubes and rub them in with your fingertips until the mixture resembles breadcrumbs. Stir in 75 g (2½ oz) of the cheese and the spring onions. Make a well in the middle, pour in the milk and add the mustard and mix until it becomes a ragged dough. Using your hands, bring it together. Turn out onto a lightly floured work surface and knead briefly, then pat into a circle, about 2 cm (¾ in) thick. Sprinkle over the remaining cheese and lightly press into the top. Cut the dough into six triangles, like a cake.

Heat the air fryer to 180°C (350°F). Once hot, place the scone wedges in the air fryer, on the rack, spaced slightly apart. Bake for 15 minutes, or until golden and well-risen.

225 g (8 oz/generous 1¾ cups) self-raising (self-rising) flour, plus extra for dusting
1 teaspoon baking powder
pinch of salt
50 g (1¾ oz) cold unsalted butter, cubed
100 g (3½ oz) mature Cheddar cheese, grated
4 spring onions (scallions), finely chopped
100 ml (3½ fl oz/scant ½ cup) whole (full-fat) milk
1 teaspoon made English mustard

# Simple Sausage Rolls

These are my son's favourite recipe from this book. Hooray! They're very moreish as they are, but would also work with other flavourings instead of the mustard and thyme. You could add 2 teaspoons of your favourite curry paste for a spicy version and a little fresh coriander (cilantro) squished into the mix, or 2 teaspoons of pesto for an Italian flavour.

/ Makes 12 /

Unroll the pastry and cut it in half lengthways, so that you have two long strips.

In a medium bowl, mix the sausage meat with the mustard and thyme, adding a little salt and pepper as well.

Divide the sausage meat in half and form into two long thin logs, along one side of each of the pieces of puff pastry. Brush the other side of the pastry with a little of the beaten egg, then roll up from the sausage meat-side so that the pastry joins with the egg-washed side. Roll so that the join is at the bottom of the sausage roll. Cut each roll into six equal pieces, score with a sharp knife and brush the tops with more beaten egg. The sausage rolls can now be chilled and baked later or baked straight away in batches.

Heat the air fryer to 200°C (400°F). Once hot, bake on the rack in two batches for 12–15 minutes until puffed and golden.

320 g (10¾ oz) sheet ready-rolled puff pastry
400 g (14 oz) pork sausage meat
2 teaspoons English mustard
1 teaspoon dried thyme
salt and freshly ground black pepper
1 egg, beaten

# 'Cornish'-style Pasties

OK, so these are square for simplicity and convenience, but they're still filled with classic Cornish pasty ingredients. They can be made ahead, chilled and baked later, if you like.

/ Makes 4 /

Add the swede, potato and onion to a food processor and whizz to finely chop. You could do this by hand, but I'm too lazy, the processor is quicker and easier! Transfer to a large bowl, then stir in the mustard and season well.

Slice the steak as thinly as you can, then cut into smaller pieces. Mix this with the vegetables.

Unroll the pastry and with the long side facing you, cut it into four equal strips. Using a rolling pin, give each piece a quick roll widthways to make the pastry a little thinner and wider. Divide the steak and vegetable mix over one side of each piece, leaving an edge of about 1 cm (½ in) around the three outer sides. Brush the edges with the beaten egg, then bring the other half of the pastry over the top of the filling. Press the edges together and crimp with your fingers or a fork, then brush the tops with more beaten egg.

Heat the air fryer to 160°C (325°F). Once hot, place a piece of baking parchment that fits your air fryer on the rack and top with the pasties. Bake for 20 minutes, then remove the baking parchment and bake for another 5 minutes to make sure the base of the pasties are cooked. You'll probably need to bake two at a time. They can be eaten hot or cold.

150 g (5½ oz) swede (rutabaga), peeled and roughly chopped
150 g (5½ oz) potato, peeled and roughly chopped
1 small onion (about 50 g/1¾ oz), peeled and roughly chopped
1 tablespoon English mustard
salt and freshly ground black pepper
200 g (7 oz) piece sirloin steak
457 g (17 oz) ready-rolled shortcrust pastry
1 egg, beaten

# Sweet Spiced Carrot Tart

These days, most ready-made brands of puff pastry are vegan, which is excellent news when it comes to baking savoury treats for friends who are plant-based. This tart, however, is a hit with both vegans and omnivores! The size of this pastry fits my air fryer perfectly, but cut your pastry to the size you need. Use any leftover pastry to make the Cheese Straws on page 107.

/ Serves 2 /

Heat the air fryer to 180°C (350°F). In a large bowl, toss the onion and carrots with the caraway and nigella seeds, the olive oil and some salt and pepper. Once the air fryer is up to temperature, add the carrot mixture and cook for 20 minutes. After this time the carrots should be pretty much done and the onion turning crispy in places. Return the mixture to the bowl and toss with the maple syrup.

Score a thin edge, about 5 mm (¼ in), around the edge of the pastry.

Place the pastry on a sheet of baking parchment and place on the shelf of the air fryer. Bake for 10 minutes, then open the drawer and press the middle of the pastry down, so that the risen scored edge is left. Pile the carrot mixture into the middle of the pastry and return to the air fryer for 5 minutes.

Meanwhile, to make the sauce, stir the tahini, yoghurt, garlic and water together in a bowl and season to taste. Once the tart is baked, drizzle with the tahini sauce and scatter with the parsley leaves. Serve.

1 red onion, sliced
6 small carrots, about 350–400g (12–14 oz) carrots, sliced lengthways into quarters
1 teaspoon caraway seeds
1 teaspoon nigella seeds
1 tablespoon olive oil
salt and freshly ground black pepper
1 tablespoon maple syrup
ready-made puff pastry sheet, cut to 14 x 23.5 cm (5½ x 9¼ in)
small handful of parsley leaves, to garnish

FOR THE SAUCE
1 tablespoon tahini
2 tablespoons plant-based plain yoghurt
1 small garlic clove, finely grated
1 tablespoon water

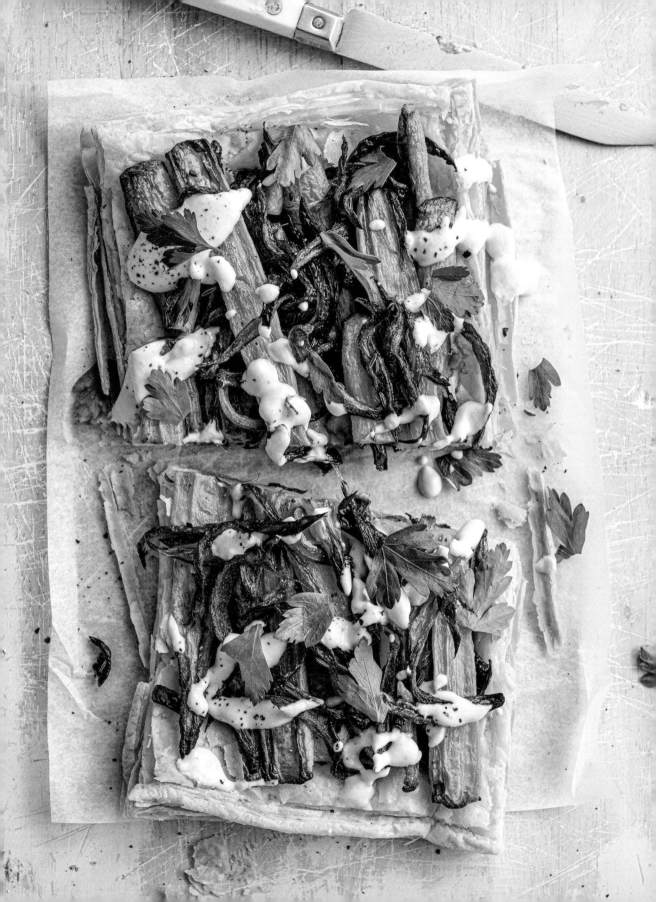

# Gougères

These savoury choux buns are great as a nibble served with drinks, or just as a lovely snack. I've used Gruyère but any strong cheese would work. Make sure you weigh the water and milk, it makes all the difference.

/ Makes about 18 /

Sift the flour onto a sheet of baking parchment.

Heat the milk, butter, a good pinch of salt and the water in a saucepan over a medium heat until the butter is melted. Increase the heat and, once the liquid is boiling, using the baking parchment as a chute, quickly pour the flour into the pan. Beat well until the mixture is smooth, then remove from the heat and leave for 10–15 minutes until it has just come to room temperature.

Once cooled slightly, using a wooden spoon or silicone spatula, beat the eggs, one by one, into the mixture followed by all of the cheese, except for 1 tablespoon.

Fit a piping bag with a large round nozzle and pipe blobs the size of a walnut onto a sheet of baking parchment that will fit your air fryer. Sprinkle the reserved cheese over the top.

Heat the air fryer to 160°C (325°F). Once hot, bake the gougères on the rack in batches for 20 minutes, or until puffed and golden.

60 g (2 oz/½ cup) plain (all-purpose) flour
60 g (2 oz/¼ cup) whole (full-fat) milk
50 g (1¾ oz) unsalted butter
pinch of salt
60 g (2 oz/¼ cup) water
2 eggs
60 g (2 oz) Gruyère or other strong cheese, grated

# Cheese and Bacon Quiche

This quiche is great served warm with a green salad and maybe some air fryer chips, but it's also perfect for lunchboxes, so worth saving a slice or two for the next day!

/ Cuts into 6–8 /

Preheat the air fryer to 200°C (400°F). Once hot, add the pancetta and cook for 5 minutes, or until browned. Remove from the air fryer and leave to cool.

Turn a 20 cm (8 in) sandwich cake tin (pan) over and press over a piece of kitchen foil, pressing it to the shape of the tin. Turn over again and put the foil into the right side of the tin, it should fit perfectly. Unroll the pastry and use to line the foil-lined tin, pressing the pastry into the edges. Chill in the refrigerator for 20 minutes.

Once the pastry has chilled, heat the air fryer to 180°C (350°F). Line the pastry case with a piece of baking parchment and fill with baking beans or dry rice. Bake for 10 minutes, then remove the baking beans or rice and bake for another 10 minutes.

In a medium bowl, beat the eggs with the cream, then season. Sprinkle the bacon and cheese into the baked pastry case and pour over the cream mixture. Return to the air fryer, cover with foil and bake for 20 minutes. Remove the foil and then bake for another 10 minutes. The quiche should be golden and just firm to the touch. Serve warm or cold.

200 g (7 oz) cubed smoked pancetta or smoked lardons
320 g (11½ oz) ready-rolled shortcrust pastry
2 eggs
200 ml (7 fl oz/scant 1 cup) double (heavy) cream
salt and freshly ground black pepper
75 g (2½ oz) Gruyère, grated

# Cheese Straws

This classic party snack is a great way of using up any leftover bits of puff pastry. If you have any little bits of hard cheeses like Red Leicester or Parmesan you need to use up then chuck them in too.

**/ Makes 14 /**

Unroll the puff pastry so that the long side is facing you, then brush all over with the beaten egg. Scatter on the grated cheeses, grind over the black pepper to cover, then press the cheeses into the pastry so they are well stuck. Cut the pastry vertically into 2 cm (¾ in) thick strips and twist each a couple of times. Brush again with any leftover beaten egg.

Heat the air fryer to 160°C (325°F). Once hot, bake the straws in batches, on the rack, for 15 minutes, or until golden and puffed.

320 g (10¾ oz) ready-rolled puff pastry
1 egg, beaten
75 g (2½ oz) mature Cheddar, grated
75 g (2½ oz) Gruyère, grated
freshly ground black pepper

# Mini Calzones

I love these little pizzas and they are a big hit with kids. I've used pepperoni in mine, but if you'd prefer it to be meat-free, swap that out for a few slices of courgette (zucchini).

/ Makes 4 /

To make the dough, add the flour, yeast, sugar and salt to a large bowl and make a well in the middle. Gradually add the tepid water, mixing as you go. Once the dough has come together to form a craggy ball, still with some dry bits, tip it out onto a work surface and, using clean hands, bring it together. Once together, knead for 5 minutes, or until smooth. You shouldn't need to add more flour, but if the dough is sticking to the work surface then add just a little.

Grease a large, lidded container or a bowl with a little olive oil and place the dough ball inside. Cover and leave to rise in a warm place for 45–60 minutes until the dough has doubled in size.

Once the dough has risen, knock it back, then rub with a little more oil and divide the dough into four balls. Leave on the work surface, or a cutting board, covered with a dish towel, to prove for 30 minutes.

Roll out each ball of dough to a 20 cm (8 in) round. Spread half of each round with 2 tablespoons passata, leaving around a 1 cm (½ in) space of dough around the edge. Top the passata with four slices of pepperoni, a quarter of the cheeses and a little basil. Brush the edges of the dough with water and fold the uncovered half over the filling. Twist the rounded edge together to seal. Brush with the remaining oil.

Preheat the air fryer to 180°C (350°F). Add two calzones to the basket and cook for 10 minutes, or until golden and puffed. Cook the next two calzones in the same way. Leave to cool slightly before tucking in.

250 g (9 oz/2 cups) plain (all-purpose) flour
7 g (¼ oz) sachet fast-action dried yeast
1 teaspoon caster (superfine) sugar
1 teaspoon fine sea salt
150 ml (5 fl oz/scant ⅔ cup) tepid water
2 tablespoons olive oil
8 tablespoons passata
16 slices pepperoni
100 g (3½ oz) firm mozzarella, grated
50 g (1¾ oz) Cheddar, grated
handful of basil leaves, torn

# Cheese and Garlic Tear and Share

This recipes uses my go-to dough when I want a super easy bread for filling with delicious flavours. The plain flour doesn't need lots of kneading like a strong flour and the results are soft and lovely.

/ Tears into 8 /

To make the dough, add the flour, yeast, sugar and sea salt to a large bowl and make a well in the middle. Gradually add the tepid water, mixing as you go. Once the dough has come together to form a craggy ball, still with some dry bits, tip it out onto a work surface and, using clean hands, bring it together. Once together, knead for 5 minutes, or until smooth. You shouldn't need to add more flour, but if the dough is sticking to the work surface then add just a little.

Grease a large lidded container or a bowl with a little olive oil and place the dough ball inside. Cover and leave to rise in a warm place for 45–60 minutes until the dough has doubled in size.

Meanwhile, prepare the filling by mixing the cheeses, parsley and garlic together in a small bowl.

Oil a 900 g (2 lb) loaf tin (pan). Once the dough has risen, turn it out onto a lightly oiled work surface and roll it out to a 30 x 30 cm (12 x 12 in) square, then spread over the cheese mixture. Start to roll up from one end (it doesn't matter which as it's a square). Brush a little water on the opposite end and roll so that the join is underneath the roll. Cut into eight pieces and arrange with the spirals facing up in the prepared loaf tin. Cover and leave in a warm place to prove for 30 minutes, or until the dough has puffed up.

Heat the air fryer to 160°C (325°F). Drizzle the bread with the 1 tablespoon oil and dot each spiral with a little of the butter, then bake for 25–30 minutes until golden and risen.

250 g (9 oz/2 cups) plain (all-purpose) flour
7 g (¼ oz) sachet fast-action dried yeast
1 teaspoon caster (superfine) sugar
1 teaspoon fine sea salt
150 ml (5 fl oz/scant ⅔ cup) tepid water
1 tablespoon olive oil, plus extra for greasing
50 g (1¾ oz) mozzarella, grated
50 g (1¾ oz) Cheddar, grated
10 g (½ oz) parsley leaves, finely chopped
4 garlic cloves, finely chopped
10 g (½ oz) butter

# Turkish-style Pide Pizza

These little pizza-style breads are a lovely alternative to Italian pizza flavours – spicy and fragrant, with a lovely tang of salty feta! They would also work as four smaller versions to serve as a starter maybe with a little rocket (arugula) and a drizzle of tahini.

/ Makes 2 /

To make the dough, add the flour, yeast, sugar and sea salt to a large bowl and make a well in the middle. Gradually add the tepid water, mixing as you go. Once the dough has come together to form a craggy ball, still with some dry bits, tip it out onto a work surface and, using clean hands, bring it together. Once together, knead for 5 minutes, or until smooth. You shouldn't need to add more flour, but if the dough is sticking to the work surface then add just a little.

Grease a large lidded container or a bowl with a little olive oil and place the dough ball inside. Cover and leave to rise in a warm place for 45–60 minutes until the dough has doubled in size.

Meanwhile, to make the lamb filling, heat 1 tablespoon of the oil in a frying pan (skillet) over a medium heat. Add the onion and cook for a few minutes, or until softened. Stir in the meat, breaking it up with a wooden spoon, and cook until browned. Stir in the garlic, herbs and spices and cook for another minute or two, then stir in the tomato purée and a splash of water. Cook together for another few minutes, then season and stir in the diced pepper. Set aside.

Once the dough has risen, knock it back and divide it in half. Using your hands, press the dough out into an

continued overleaf

250 g (9 oz/2 cups) plain (all-purpose) flour
7 g (¼ oz) sachet fast-action dried yeast
1 teaspoon caster (superfine) sugar
1 teaspoon fine sea salt
150 ml (5 fl oz/scant ⅔ cup) tepid water
2 tablespoons olive oil, plus extra for greasing
½ onion, finely chopped
250 g (9 oz) lamb mince (ground lamb)
1 garlic clove, crushed, or finely grated
½ teaspoon each ground cinnamon, ground cumin, ground coriander, Turkish chilli (pul biber), sumac and dried mint
2 tablespoons tomato purée (paste)
salt and freshly ground black pepper
½ green (bell) pepper, finely diced
50 g (1¾ oz) feta, crumbled
finish with fresh mint and chilli flakes, to scatter

oval shape and place on a piece of baking parchment. Spread half the lamb mixture over each oval, leaving a little gap at the edges. Bring up the sides around the filling and twist the ends together to make points. Drizzle with the remaining oil.

Heat the air fryer to 190°C (375°F). Place one pide in at a time on the baking parchment on the rack – mine go in diagonally – and bake on the parchment for 6–7 minutes. Remove the parchment and bake for another 2–3 minutes. Repeat with the second pide. Sprinkle with the feta and mint leaves and scatter over a little more chilli flakes, if liked.

# Red Onion and Cheese Rolls

These veggie rolls are a nice alternative to sausage rolls and great for a buffet when you're feeding a crowd. They're lovely warm or cold.

/ Makes 12 /

Heat the butter and oil in a frying pan (skillet) until the butter has melted. Add the red onion with a pinch of salt and the sugar and cook over a medium-low heat for about 15 minutes, stirring occasionally until the onion is softened and beginning to brown a little. Transfer to a large bowl and leave to cool.

Once the onions have cooled, add the breadcrumbs, cheese, one egg, a pinch of salt and a good grind of black pepper to the bowl and mix well.

Unroll the pastry and cut it in half lengthways so that you have two long strips. Spread the cheese mixture down one long side of each piece of pastry in a sausage shape. Beat the remaining egg in a small bowl, then brush the edges of the pastry with some of the beaten egg and roll up starting from the side with the cheese mix on, so that the join is underneath the roll. Press together gently, then cut each roll into six equal pieces. Brush the tops with more beaten egg and sprinkle on the onion seeds.

Heat the air fryer to 200°C (400°F). Once hot, bake in two batches on the rack for 12 minutes, or until puffed and golden.

25 g (¾ oz) butter
1 tablespoon oil
1 large red onion, thinly sliced
salt and freshly ground black pepper
pinch of sugar
50 g (1¾ oz/scant ⅔ cup) fresh breadcrumbs
250 g (9 oz) crumbly cheese, such as Caerphilly or Wensleydale or similar or Cheddar
2 eggs
320 g (10¾ oz) sheet ready-rolled puff pastry
black onions seeds, to garnish (use nigella, if liked)

# BREADS AND DOUGHS

# Chocolate Twists

My son loves a pain au chocolate. These are a great alternative to shop-bought that you can prep the night before and air fry in the morning to have warm and fresh!

/ Makes 15 /

Unroll the dough and cut along the vertical perforated lines to make three rectangles of dough. Push the horizontal perforations together.

Heat the custard in a small saucepan until just warm. In a small bowl, mix the cornflour with the hot water and stir into the custard. Heat for another 2 minutes, or until the custard is visibly thicker. Remove the pan from the heat.

With the dough rectangles on the work surface with the short sides facing you, spread the custard over the bottom halves of each piece of dough, then evenly sprinkle over the chocolate chips. Pull the uncovered side of the dough over the top of the chocolate and custard and push the halves together (you may need to lightly flour your hands).

Heat the air fryer to 160°C (325°F). Once hot, cut each filled rectangle into five small pieces and bake for 8–10 minutes until golden and puffed. Remove from the air fryer and dust with icing sugar.

340 g (11¼ oz) pack ready-made croissant dough
100 g (3½ oz) ready-made custard
1 heaped teaspoon cornflour (cornstarch)
1 teaspoon hot water
100 g (3½ oz/scant ⅔ cup) chocolate chips
flour, for dusting
icing (powdered) sugar, for dusting

# Cinnamon Rolls

Home made cinnamon buns are often made with an enriched dough, which can be a little bit of effort. These rolls, using my easy dough recipe, are so simple to make and drizzled with the creamy icing and served just warm they're a real treat.

/ Makes 8 /

To make the dough, put the flour, yeast, sugar and salt into a mixing bowl and make a well in the centre. Gradually add the water, mixing as you go. Once the dough has come together to form a craggy ball, still with some dry bits, tip it out onto a work surface and with clean hands bring together. Once together knead for around 5 minutes, until the mix is smooth. You shouldn't need to add more flour, but if the dough is sticking to the work surface then add just a little.

Grease a large lidded container or bowl with a little oil and place the dough ball inside. Cover and leave to rise in a warm place for 45 minutes–1 hour, or until doubled in size.

While the dough rises, prepare the filling; squash together the soft butter with the cinnamon and sugar until it is a brown spreadable mixture. If the butter is a bit hard then pop it into the microwave for 10–15 seconds to just soften it slightly.

Once the dough is doubled, turn out onto a lightly oiled counter and roll to a 30 x 30 cm (12 x 12 in) square and spread over the soft butter mixture. Start to roll up from one end (it doesn't matter which as it's a square). Brush a little water on the opposite end and roll so that the join is underneath the roll. Cut into 8 pieces and arrange with the spirals up in a buttered 900 g (2 lb) loaf tin. Cover and leave in a warm place for around 30 minutes, until the dough is puffed up.

Heat the air fryer to 160°C (325°F) and once hot bake for 25–30 minutes, until golden and risen. Leave to cool in the tin for 5 minutes, or until you can handle it, then place on a serving plate. Mix the icing sugar with the milk and drizzle over the buns.

250 g (9 oz/2 cups) plain (all-purpose) flour
7 g (¼ oz) sachet fast-action dried yeast
1 teaspoon caster (superfine) sugar
1 teaspoon fine sea salt
150 ml (5 fl oz/scant ⅔ cup) tepid water
50 g (2 oz) softened unsalted butter, plus extra for greasing
1 teaspoon ground cinnamon
75 g (2½ oz) soft brown sugar
6 tablespoons icing (powdered) sugar
1 tablespoon milk

# Antipasti-stuffed Focaccia

I've been making versions of this bread for years so was curious to see if it would transfer successfully to the air fryer and of course it did. It's super easy and always so popular that it gets devoured as soon as it's not too hot to hold!

/ Serves 4–6 /

Add the flour, fine salt and yeast to a large bowl and stir together. Make a well in the centre and gradually add the water, stirring to form a dough (you may not need all the water, or you may need a tiny bit more to make the dough come together). Using your hands, bring the dough together, picking up any dry or sticky bits around the sides of the bowl.

Lightly flour a work surface and turn out the dough. Knead for 5–10 minutes until the dough is smooth and elastic. Oil the bowl you made the dough in and add the dough, then cover and leave to rise for 45–60 minutes until doubled in size.

Once the dough has doubled in size, lightly oil a piece of baking parchment and turn the dough out onto it. Using your hands, press the dough into a rectangle, about 30 x 25 cm (12 x 10 in). Spread the artichokes, sundried tomatoes, olives and basil over half of the dough, then sprinkle with 2 tablespoons of the Parmesan and drizzle with 2 teaspoons of the oil from the sundried tomatoes, or the artichokes. Fold the other half of the dough over the top of the filling and tuck underneath the bottom to seal. Slide onto a baking tray (pan), cover and leave to prove for 20–30 minutes until puffed up.

Heat the air fryer to 200°C (400°F). Once the dough is ready, transfer to the rack of the air fryer, still on the baking parchment. Press holes into the top of the dough, drizzle with a little more oil from the tomato jar and sprinkle with the remaining Parmesan and some flaky salt. Bake for 15 minutes, or until risen and golden. Check that the base is cooked and if it is still a little underdone, turn over and return to the air fryer for another 5 minutes. Leave to cool for as long as you're able to before slicing and devouring!

250 g (9 oz/2 cups) strong white flour, plus extra for dusting
5 g (¼ oz) fine sea salt
1 teaspoon fast-action dried yeast
175 ml (6 fl oz/¾ cup) water
6 pieces artichoke in olive oil, cut lengthways
6 sundried tomatoes, chopped, plus a little of the oil
8 black olives, sliced
handful of basil leaves, shredded
3 tablespoons grated Parmesan
flaky sea salt, for sprinkling

# White Loaf

There is nothing more satisfying than a simple loaf of white bread, especially if it's fresh from the air fryer and smothered in butter.

/ Makes 1 loaf /

Add the flour, yeast, sugar and salt to a large bowl. Stir together, then make a well in the centre. Add the oil, then gradually add the water, stirring to form a dough (you may not need all the water, or you may need a tiny bit more to make the dough come together). Using your hands, bring the dough together, picking up any dry or sticky bits around the sides of the bowl.

Lightly flour a work surface and turn out the dough. Knead for 5–10 minutes until the dough is smooth and elastic. Oil the bowl you used to make the bread in or oil a lidded container. Pop in the dough, cover and leave to rise for 45–60 minutes until doubled in size.

Once the dough has doubled in size, knock it back and shape it into an oval. Transfer the dough to a piece of baking parchment and leave to prove for 30 minutes, or until puffed up.

Heat the air fryer to 200°C (400°F). Once hot, add the bread to the air fryer, still on the baking parchment, and bake for 10 minutes. Reduce the heat to 180°C (350°F) and bake for another 10 minutes. After this time, the bread will look done, but still needs a little more baking. Turn the loaf over and bake for another 5 minutes. The bread will be baked when it sounds hollow on the bottom when you tap it with your finger. Leave to cool completely before tucking in.

450 g (1 lb/3⅔ cups) strong white bread flour, plus extra for dusting
7 g (¼ oz) sachet fast-action dried yeast
1 teaspoon caster (superfine) sugar
10 g (½ oz) fine sea salt
1 tablespoon olive oil, plus extra for greasing
300 ml (10 fl oz/1¼ cups) water

# Toad in the Hole

Being from Yorkshire, I do love anything made with Yorkshire pudding mix, particularly toad in the hole, which always has a nice combination of crisp batter edges with thick pancakey bits in the middle.

/ Serves 2–3 /

Put the sausages and oil into a 20 cm (8 in) square cake tin, or similar that fits your air fryer. Heat the air fryer to 200°C (400°F) and once hot put the tin in and cook for 5 minutes.

Whizz together the flour, pinch nutmeg, milk, eggs and a pinch of salt in a high speed blender (the kind you make smoothies in). If you don't have a blender like this then in a jug beat the eggs into the milk. Add the flour to a small mixing bowl and gradually beat the milk mixture into the flour and nutmeg, then season.

After 5 minutes, open the air fryer and pour the batter into the hot tin, over and around the sausages. Return to cook for another 10–15 minutes, until the sausages are browned and the batter puffed and golden.

4–6 pork sausages
3 tablespoons vegetable oil
75 g (3 oz/⅔ cup) plain (all-purpose) flour
pinch of ground nutmeg
100 ml (3½ fl oz/scant ½ cup) whole milk
2 eggs
pinch of salt

# Dutch Baby

This is an American-style breakfast dish that combines sweet and savoury elements, but if you'd prefer it just sweet then omit the bacon and serve with the blueberries and maple syrup.

/ Serves 2 /

Add the milk, flour, sugar, eggs, and vanilla to a high-speed blender and whizz to a smooth batter. I find this works well in a small high speed blender (the kind you make smoothies in) but if you don't have one then this can be made in a bowl. Add the flour and sugar to a bowl, make a well in the centre and beat in the milk, eggs and vanilla until you have a smooth batter.

Heat the air fryer to 200°C (400°F) with a 20 cm (8 in) sandwich tin (pan) inside. The tin itself needs to be hot. Once hot, carefully add the butter to the tin and, using a silicone spatula, swirl around to melt. Once the butter is melted, pour in the batter and cook for 4–5 minutes. At this point the baby should be puffed up. Add the bacon to the middle and cook for another 4–5 minutes (set the air fryer to 10 minutes at the start).

After 9–10 minutes, the dutch baby should be well puffed and the bacon becoming golden. Carefully remove from the air fryer, tumble on blueberries, if you like, and drizzle with maple syrup. Divide between two or just get stuck in together from the same plate!

75 ml (2½ fl oz/5 tablespoons) whole milk
50 g (1¾ oz/generous ⅓ cup) plain (all-purpose) flour
1 tablespoon caster (superfine) sugar
2 medium eggs
½ teaspoon vanilla extract
15 g (½ oz) butter
4 slices of smoked streaky bacon
handful of blueberries (optional)
maple syrup, for drizzling

# Umami Soda Bread

This is a super-quick bread that you can knock together in minutes, and the yeast extract gives it a brilliant umami kick.

/ Makes 1 loaf /

Sift both flours into a large bowl. Stir in the bicarbonate of soda, then make a well in the centre and pour in the buttermilk and dissolved yeast extract. Stir well to form a craggy dough. Bring this dough together with your hands, then turn out onto a lightly floured work surface and knead briefly into a ball. Using a sharp knife, score a cross in the top.

Heat the air fryer to 180°C (350°F). Arrange a piece of baking parchment or a reusable silicone mat in the air fryer, then add the bread and bake for 20 minutes. Turn over and bake for another 10 minutes.

150 g (5½ oz/1¼ cups) plain (all-purpose) flour, plus extra for dusting
150 g (5½ oz/1 cup) wholemeal flour
1½ teaspoons bicarbonate of soda (baking soda)
200 g (7 oz) buttermilk or plain yoghurt
2 tablespoons yeast extract dissolved in 2 tablespoons hot water

# Seeded Wholemeal Bread

I love a seedy wholemeal loaf and making your own at home means you can add whatever seeds you fancy. I like a mix, but you could just use one kind of seed if you prefer. Nuts and dried fruit also work well in this loaf. Serve with cheese and your favourite chutney for a simple lunch or snack.

/ Makes 1 loaf /

Add the flours, yeast, salt and sugar to a large bowl. Stir together and make a well in the centre. Add the oil, then gradually add the water, stirring to form a dough (you may not need all the water, or you may need a tiny bit more to make the dough come together). Using your hands, bring the dough together, picking up any dry or sticky bits around the sides of the bowl.

Lightly flour a work surface and turn out the dough. Knead for 5–10 minutes until the dough is smooth and elastic. Oil the bowl you used to make the bread in or oil a lidded container. Pop in the dough, cover and leave to rise for 45–60 minutes until doubled in size.

Once the dough has doubled in size, knock it back and knead in the seeds. This will seem tricky, but keep going, as they will incorporate into the dough! Shape the dough into an oval, then transfer to a piece of baking parchment and leave to prove for 30 minutes, or until puffed up.

Heat the air fryer to 200°C (400°F). Once hot, add the bread to the air fryer, still on the baking parchment, and bake for 10 minutes. Reduce the heat to 180°C (350°F) and bake for another 10 minutes. After this the bread will look done, but still needs a little more baking. Turn the loaf over and bake for another 5–10 minutes. The bread will be baked when it sounds hollow on the bottom when you tap it with your finger. Leave to cool completely before tucking in.

300 g (10½ oz/2 cups) strong wholemeal or multigrain flour
100 g (3½ oz/generous ¾ cup) strong white flour, plus extra for dusting
7 g (¼ oz) sachet fast-action dried yeast
10 g (½ oz) fine salt
1 teaspoon caster (superfine) sugar
1 tablespoon olive oil
250–300 ml (8–10 fl oz/1–1¼ cups) water
75 g (2½ oz/⅔ cup) mixed seeds

# No-knead Bread Rolls

These are incredibly easy and super soft. They work really well as buns for sliders or as rolls for a dinner party.

/ Makes 9 /

Pour the milk into a medium saucepan and heat until just warm at the edges. Pour into a large bowl, then sprinkle on the yeast. Leave to stand for 2 minutes, or until the yeast has started to froth, then stir in the sugar, 30 g (1¼ oz) of the butter, salt and egg. Beat everything together, then stir in the flour and mix until it becomes a sticky dough. Drizzle the top with a little of the melted butter, then cover and leave in a warm place for 30 minutes, or until doubled in size.

Once the dough has risen, turn out onto a floured work surface and divide into nine pieces. Roll each piece into a ball. Using more of the melted butter, grease a 20 cm (8 in) square baking tin (pan), then pop in the rolls. Brush again with butter, cover and leave to prove for about 30 minutes.

Heat the air fryer to 180°C (350°F). Once hot, transfer the tin to the air fryer and bake for 30 minutes, checking after 15 minutes and covering with kitchen foil if they are browning too much.

200 ml (7 fl oz/scant 1 cup) milk
7 g (¼ oz) sachet fast-action dried yeast
20 g (¾ oz/1 heaped tablespoon) caster (superfine) sugar
45 g (13/4 oz) butter, melted
½ teaspoon salt
1 egg
375 g (12½ oz) plain (all-purpose) flour, plus extra for dusting

# Hot Cross Buns

Making your own traditional hot cross buns is a lovely weekend activity, but I've tried to make these as easy as I can, so that you'll want to make them again and again, whether it's Easter or not.

/ Makes 4 /

Add the milk and butter to a small saucepan and heat gently over a low heat until the butter has melted.

Add all the dry ingredients to a large bowl and make a well in the centre. Add half the beaten egg and the melted butter and milk mixture and stir together, then using your hands, bring it all together. Once a dough has formed, tip the mixture out onto a clean work surface, dusted with a very little amount of flour, and knead for 10 minutes, or until the dough is smooth.

Lightly oil a bowl or lidded plastic container, add the dough and cover. Leave in a warm place to rise for 1 hour, or until doubled in size.

Once the dough has risen, knock it back, then turn it out onto a work surface and knead in the dried fruit. Divide the dough into four portions and form into balls. Arrange in a square baking tin (pan) that fits your air fryer, cover and leave to prove until doubled in size.

Once the buns have doubled in size, brush with the remaining egg. Mix the remaining flour and the water together in a small bowl, then spoon into a piping bag fitted with a small nozzle or sandwich bag with a tiny bit of the end snipped off and pipe crosses on top.

Heat the air fryer to 180°C (350°F). Once hot, bake for 15 minutes. The hot cross buns should be shiny and dark brown.

100 ml (3½ fl oz/scant ½ cup) whole milk
40 g (1½ oz) unsalted butter
1 teaspoon fast-action dried yeast
25 g (¾ oz/2 tablespoons) caster (superfine) sugar
225 g (8 oz/generous 1¾ cups) strong white bread flour, plus extra for dusting
pinch of fine sea salt
1–2 teaspoons mixed spice
½ teaspoon nutmeg
½ teaspoon ground cinnamon
1 egg, beaten
oil, for greasing
75 g (2½ oz/scant ½ cup) mixed dried fruit

FOR THE CROSS
1 tablespoon plain (all-purpose) flour
2 teaspoons water

# Index

# About the Author

After working in Japan for five years, Katy returned to the UK to train as a chef at Leiths School of Food and Wine. This led to her landing her dream job at BBC Good Food magazine, and since then she has worked in the industry for almost 20 years, as a food stylist and recipe writer on pretty much every food magazine in the UK, as well as creating recipes for national supermarkets, food styling for cook books and websites and all sorts of random food related jobs in between. She lives in London with her husband and son and is often found distributing her bakes to neighbours and friends.

# Acknowledgements

I am eternally grateful to my friend Kate, without whom this book would not have happened and to Eve, for giving me a shot! Massive thanks to everyone who worked on the shoot, Ant for his always beautiful photography and for being an all round great bloke to work with, Hannah for her beautiful props and Christina and Kristine for assisting me and making it a fun shoot. Thank you Nikki for the spectacular design of the book, I love it! Thanks also to my mum and dad, brother Joe and his family, who, though not living local to me gave great feedback on the bakes I drove to Doncaster and demanded they critique! Lastly, to Dave and Freddie, one of whom tried everything I tested, the other... a few bits here and there... thank you for all your love and support!

Published in 2024 by Hardie Grant
Books (London)

Hardie Grant Books (London)
5th & 6th Floors
52–54 Southwark Street
London SE1 1UN

hardiegrantbooks.com

British Library Cataloguing-in-
Publication Data. A catalogue record
for this book is available from the
British Library.

*Super Simple Air Fryer Baking*
ISBN: 978-1-78488-775-9

10 9 8 7 6 5 4 3 2 1

Publishing Director: Kajal Mistry
Commissioning Editor: Eve Marleau
Copy Editor: Kathy Steer
Designer: Nikki Ellis
Proofreader: Sarah Prior
Indexer: Vanessa Bird
Food stylist: Katy Greenwood
Prop stylist: Hannah Wilkinson
Photographer: Ant Duncan
Production Controller: Gary Hayes

Colour reproduction by p2d
Printed in China by RR Donnelley Asia
Printing Solution Limited

FSC
www.fsc.org

MIX
Paper | Supporting
responsible forestry
FSC® C018179